Gender and the
Politics of Possibilities

D0810774

THE GENDER LENS SERIES

Series Editors

Judith A. Howard, *University of Washington*

Barbara Risman, *University of Illinois, Chicago*

Joey Sprague, *University of Kansas*

The Gender Lens series has been conceptualized as a way of encouraging the development of a sociological understanding of gender. A "gender lens" means working to make gender visible in social phenomena; asking if, how, and why social processes, standards, and opportunities differ systematically for women and men. It also means recognizing that gender inequality is inextricably braided with other systems of inequality. The Gender Lens series is committed to social change directed toward eradicating these inequalities. Originally published by Sage Publications and Pine Forge Press, all Gender Lens books are now available from The Rowman & Littlefield Publishing Group.

BOOKS IN THE SERIES

Judith A. Howard and Jocelyn A. Hollander, *Gendered Situations, Gendered Selves: A Gender Lens on Social Psychology*
Michael A. Messner, *Politics of Masculinities: Men in Movements*
Judith Lorber, *Gender and the Social Construction of Illness*
Scott Coltrane, *Gender and Families*
Myra Marx Ferree, Judith Lorber, and Beth B. Hess, editors, *Revisioning Gender*
Pepper Schwartz and Virginia Rutter, *The Gender of Sexuality: Exploring Sexual Possibilities*
Francesca M. Cancian and Stacey J. Oliker, *Caring and Gender*
M. Bahati Kuumba, *Gender and Social Movements*
Toni M. Calasanti and Kathleen F. Slevin, *Gender, Social Inequities, and Aging*
Judith Lorber and Lisa Jean Moore, *Gender and the Social Construction of Illness, Second Edition*
Shirley A. Hill, *Black Intimacies: A Gender Perspective on Families and Relationships*
Lisa D. Brush, *Gender and Governance*
Dorothy E. Smith, *Institutional Ethnography: A Sociology for People*
Joey Sprague, *Feminist Methodologies for Critical Researchers: Bridging Differences*
Joan Acker, *Class Questions: Feminist Answers*
Oriel Sullivan, *Changing Gender Relations, Changing Families: Tracing the Pace of Change over Time*
Sara L. Crawley, Lara J. Foley, and Constance L. Shehan, *Gendering Bodies*
Yen Le Espiritu, *Asian American Women and Men: Labor, Laws, and Love*
Scott Coltrane and Michele Adams, *Gender and Families, Second Edition*
Manisha Desai, *Gender and the Politics of Possibilities*

Gender and the Politics of Possibilities

Rethinking Globalization

Manisha Desai

ROWMAN & LITTLEFIELD PUBLISHERS, INC.
Lanham • Boulder • New York • Toronto • Plymouth, UK

ROWMAN & LITTLEFIELD PUBLISHERS, INC.

Published in the United States of America
by Rowman & Littlefield Publishers, Inc.
A wholly owned subsidary of The Rowman & Littlefield Publishing Group, Inc.
4501 Forbes Boulevard, Suite 200, Lanham, Maryland 20706
www.rowmanlittlefield.com

Estover Road
Plymouth PL6 7PY
United Kingdom

Copyright © 2009 by Rowman & Littlefield Publishers, Inc.

All rights reserved. No part of this publication may be reproduced,
stored in a retrieval system, or transmitted in any form or by any
means, electronic, mechanical, photocopying, recording, or otherwise,
without the prior permission of the publisher.

British Library Cataloguing in Publication Information Available

Library of Congress Cataloging-in-Publication Data:

Desai, Manisha.
  Gender and the politics of possibilities : rethinking globalization / Manisha Desai.
    p. cm. — (The gender lens series)
  Includes bibliographical references.
  ISBN-13: 978-0-7425-6377-3 (cloth : alk. paper)
  ISBN-10: 0-7425-6377-4 (cloth : alk. paper)
  ISBN-13: 978-0-7425-6378-0 (pbk. : alk. paper)
  ISBN-10: 0-7425-6378-2 (pbk. : alk. paper)
  eISBN-13: 978-0-7425-6515-9
  eISBN-10: 0-7425-6515-7
  1. Sex role and globalization. 2. Women—Employment. 3. Feminism—
International cooperation. 4. Internet and women. I. Title.
  HQ1075.D463 2008
  303.48'2082—dc22   2008025198

Printed in the United States of America

♾™ The paper used in this publication meets the minimum requirements of
American National Standard for Information Sciences—Permanence of Paper for
Printed Library Materials, ANSI/NISO Z39.48-1992.

For Nana (my dad), 1932–2005,
who first taught me about possibilities

Contents

Series Editors' Foreword

It is now more than twenty years since feminist sociologists identified gender as an important analytic dimension in sociology. In the intervening decades, theory and research on gender have grown exponentially. With this series, we intend to further this scholarship, as well as ensure that theory and research on gender become fully integrated into the discipline as a whole.

In their classic edited collection *Analyzing Gender: A Handbook of Social Science Research* (1987), Beth Hess and Myra Marx Ferree identify three stages in the study of women and men since 1970. Initially, the emphasis was on sex differences and the extent to which such differences might be based on the biological properties of individuals. In the second stage, the focus shifted to the individual sex roles and socialization, exposing gender as the product of specific social arrangements, although still conceptualizing it as an individual trait. The hallmark of the third stage is the recognition of the centrality of gender as an organizing principle in all social systems, including work, politics, everyday interaction, families, economic development, law, education, and a host of other social domains. As our understanding of gender has become more social, so has our awareness that gender is experienced and organized in race- and class-specific ways.

In the summer of 1992, the American Sociological Association (ASA) funded a small conference organized by Barbara Risman and Joey Sprague to discuss the evolution of gender in these distinctly sociological frameworks. The conference brought together a sampling of gender scholars working in a range of substantive areas with a diversity of methods to focus on gender as a principle of social organization. The discussions of the state of feminist scholarship made it clear that gender is pervasive in society and operates at multiple levels. Gender shapes identities and perception, inter-actional practices, and the very forms of social institutions, and it does so in race- and class-specific ways. If we did not see gender in social phenomena, we were not seeing them clearly.

The participants in the ASA-sponsored seminar recognized that although these developing ideas about gender were widely accepted by feminist sociologists and many others who study social inequalities, they were relatively unfamiliar to many who work within other sociological paradigms. This book series was conceived at that conference as a means of introducing these ideas to sociological colleagues and students and of helping to develop gender scholarship further.

As series editors, we believe it is time for gender scholars to speak to our other colleagues and to the general education of students. There are many sociologists and scholars in other social sciences who want to incorporate scholarship on gender and its intersections with race, class, and sexuality in their teaching and research but lack the tools to do so. For those who have not worked in this area, the prospect of the bibliographic research necessary to develop supplementary units or transform their own teaching and scholarship is daunting. Moreover, the publications necessary to penetrate a curriculum resistant to change and encumbered by inertia have simply not been available. We conceptualize this book series as a way of meeting the needs of these scholars and thereby also encouraging the development of the sociological understanding of gender by offering a "gender lens."

What do we mean by a *gender lens*? We mean working to make gender visible in social phenomena, asking if, how, and why social processes, standards, and opportunities differ systematically in women and men. We also mean recognizing that gender inequality is inextricably intertwined with other systems of inequality. Looking at the world through a gendered lens thus implies two seemingly contradictory tasks. First, it means unpacking the assumptions about gender that pervade sociological research and social life in general. At the same time, looking through a gender lens means revealing how central assumptions about gender continue to be the organization of the social world, regardless of their empirical reality. We show how our often unquestioned ideas about gender affect the words we use, the questions we ask, the answers we envision. The Gender Lens Series is committed to social change directed toward eradicating these inequalities. Our goals are consistent with initiatives at colleges and universities across the United States that are encouraging the development of more-diverse scholarship and teaching.

The books in the Gender Lens Series are aimed at different audiences and have been written for a variety of uses, from assigned readings in introductory undergraduate courses to graduate seminars and as professional resources for our colleagues. The series includes several different styles of books that address these goals in distinct ways. We are excited about the series and anticipate that it will have an enduring impact on the direction of both the pedagogy and the scholarship in sociology and other related social sciences. We invite you, the reader, to join us in thinking through these difficult but exciting issues by offering feedback or by developing your own project and proposing it for us in the series.

ABOUT THIS BOOK

In this book Manisha Desai identifies multiple processes that are typically lumped together under the rubric of globalization: economic, political, and cultural. Using a gender lens, Desai argues, illuminates how the macro as well as the micro realities of each of these globalizations are gendered. Men and women have different opportunities and barriers to engage and shape the processes of globalizations.

Mainstream accounts of globalization focus on disembodied actors such as multinational corporations, technological processes, and global institutions and often assume that these forces travel from the West to the rest; and the best that people can do in response to these forces is to resist, adapt, or face dislocation and displacement. In contrast, Desai brings into focus gendered actors around the globe and argues that these social actors are not just impacted by the various globalizations, they actively constitute these globalizations. Drawing on participant observation, interviews, documentary analysis, secondary sources, as well as a critical reading of the gender and globalizations literatures, she develops an analysis of three critical cases: cross-border traders in Africa, transnational feminists working through the UN, grassroots collaborations and via the World Social Forum, and *modemujeres* in Latin America. She shows how the practices of these social actors articulate a politics of possibilities that has shaped the global justice movements.

Desai's analyses provides a complex and nuanced picture of the gendered processes comprising globalization while it highlights the possibilities for global justice that is evident in the work of the actors who come into view using a gender lens.

Judith A. Howard
Barbara Risman
Joey Sprague

Acknowledgments

Like most endeavors, this one would not have been possible without the support of numerous colleagues, friends, and family members. My intellectual and emotional debts are many, spread over many decades, multiple institutions, and several continents, as is only appropriate given the topic at hand and the nature of our lives today.

None of this would have started without the editors of the Gender Lens Series at Rowman & Littlefield, Judith Howard, Barbara Risman, and Joey Sprague, who first asked me to write this book and who have supported me through the years. In particular, I want to acknowledge Joey Sprague for being my "madrina" and pushing me to clarify my arguments for the "guy down the hall." I hope that the book will enable many guys, down many halls, to see the gendered nature of contemporary globalizations. I would also like to thank the reviewers, Valentine Moghdam and Robert Schaeffer, for their generous comments on the manuscript. For valuable help with the bibliography, I want to thank Meltem Yilmaz-Sener at the University of Illinois; and, at the University of Connecticut, Shweta Majumdar, Jessica Monroy, and Abby Willis.

But writing, whether a book or an essay, requires not only a book contract but also uninterrupted time that one can devote to the task. For such a gift of time, I am indebted to the Women and Gender in Global Perspectives Program (WGGP) at the University of Illinois, and especially to Gale Summerfield, the director of the program, who encouraged me throughout the writing and excused me from various program responsibilities to facilitate the completion of this work. Kathy Martin, also at WGGP, has been a constant supporter during my nearly five years in the program. At the University of Connecticut, I thank Kate Hurley-Dizigan and Coleen Spurlock for their help with preparing the manuscript.

Colleagues at the University of Illinois, especially in the Transnational Seminar Series of the Sociology Department, provided constant intellectual dialogue. Behrooz Ghamari-Tabrizi, Zsuzsa Gille, Michael Goldman, Cameron McCarthy, Faranak Miraftab, Jan Nederveen Pieterse, Faisal Rizvi, Ken Salo, Mahir Saul, Markus Schulz, Rachel Schurman, Angharad Valdivia, and David Wilson have all contributed food for thought as well as for body and soul. And without the levity and libations of the numerous "girls' nights out" with Angelina Cotler, Zsuzsa Gille, Faranak Miraftab, Lisa Rosenthal, Rachel Schurman, and Angharad Valdivia, this process would not have flowed as smoothly as it did.

In India, Poornima Chikarmane, Chhaya Datar, Nandita Gandhi, Bakula Ghaswala, Miloon Kothari, Smitu Kothari, Minar Pimple, Nandita Shah, and scholar-activists too many to name have been a source of inspiration and support for decades. My dad, Nana, whose unexpected death while I was writing this book turned my world around, and to whom the book is dedicated, broke many social barriers in his day and enabled me to become a committed scholar-activist. My mum, Nirmala, and my brother, Alpesh, have always been there for me, even when they couldn't fathom what I was up to.

And, above all, my deepest gratitude to Jeremy, Ishan, and Ilan for being good humored about my travels and distractions, for reminding me about my "feminist praxis," for Jeremy's excellent editorial eye, and, most importantly, for their constant love and support.

Introduction

Women from Zimbabwe, Angola, Malawi, and other southern African countries travel between their countries and South Africa, selling crocheted work as well as bedspreads and linen, artwork, and wood carvings in South Africa, and bringing home consumer goods such as kitchen utensils, mattresses, clothes, and televisions and other electronic goods.

At any UN meeting or international conference or convention you see educated, middle-class women as well as poor, uneducated women sharing their experiences of organizing or working for nongovernmental organizations (NGOs) that work with, conduct research on, and engage in policy work for gender issues.

Modemmujers are women in Mexico who are bringing the benefits of information and communication technologies to rural women, to help them communicate with others as well as sharing their stories with others across many borders.

What do these women have in common? They represent different, perhaps conflicting, views of globalizations, as compared with what is commonly available in popular and academic analyses. They are some of the faces of contemporary globalizations that I seek to illuminate in this book. I use the plural term *globalizations*, as the nearly two decades of "globalization" scholarship has shown that economic, political, and cultural globalizations, while interconnected, are not the same, and that each involves different sets of processes (e.g., Moghadam 2005; Nederveen Pieterse 2004; Steger 2003).

By now it is a cliché to say that the term *globalization* has become ubiquitous in popular and academic discourses. Despite its ubiquity, however, there are many aspects of the processes of contemporary globalizations that remain invisible. My aim in this book is to illuminate two such invisible aspects.

First, most popular and academic analysts of globalizations focus on the macro level, that is, on how transnational corporations (TNCs) are moving their manufacturing and, increasingly, their service work across borders; or how the new communication and information technologies are making it possible for people to connect, travel, and experience events in other parts of the world in real time; or how global institutions and regimes are changing global politics. In short, the macro focus suggests that the "world is flat" (Friedman 2005). The first wave of globalization scholars (e.g., Giddens 1999; Ritzer 2004; Sklair 2002) emphasized this increasing deterritorialization, the growing interconnectedness, and a borderless world. The second wave of globalization analysts (e.g., McDonald 2006; Nederveen Pieterse 2004, 2007; Steger 2003; Urry 2003), writing in the new century are more careful and talk of complex time and complex spaces, uneven globalizations, and the peaks and valleys in the global geography.

But this bird's-eye view misses the contours and topography of the varied realities on the ground, providing an incomplete picture. By focusing on the micro, lived reality of common people, I wish not only to provide a more nuanced and complex picture, but also to highlight actors not immediately connected to globalizations by most analysts. The macro analysts of globalization not only miss the realities on the ground, they also tend to highlight disembodied actors such as multinational corporations, technological processes, and global institutions. I want to highlight how ordinary men and women are also important actors of globalizations.

Second, most analysts of globalization view it as a process emerging in the West and spreading to the rest of the world. The second-wave analysts of globalization are more careful and talk of multiple globalizations, not all emanating from the West. But the dominant view among economists and sociologists is unilinear. We see globalization moving from the West to the rest. This is a result of a narrow framing of globalization as a process of the last few decades of the twentieth century. But if one sees globalization in a "*longue durée*," then globalization, as movement of people, ideas, and goods across borders, has been part of human history from its origin (Abu-Lughod 1989; Nederveen Pieterse 2004). What is different about contemporary globalizations is their pace and scale. By being Western-centric, analysts miss important processes and practices in other parts of the world. In the view of Western-centric analysts, people in other parts of the world are impacted by the various forces of globalizations, particularly economic forces, and the best they can do is either resist, adapt, or face dislocation and displacement. By decentering the West, we can see that people not only react to globalizations, they also shape global processes by the creative and innovative ways in which they act in the contemporary conjuncture.

A gender lens is crucial to such a project of illumination, as it highlights how the macro as well as the micro realities are gendered, and how men and women have different opportunities to engage and shape the processes of globalizations and face different barriers. For example, the dis-embodied actors of globalizations, such as TNCs, information and communication technologies, and intergovernmental bodies, are not abstractions, but are mostly composed of elite men (and some women), or what Leslie Sklair (2002) calls the "transnational capitalist class." As men, they bring gendered understandings in fashioning globalizations. At the micro level, it is women, as cross-border traders, transnational activists, and *Modemmujers*, who are shaping processes of globalization in specifically gendered ways. To miss the ways in which both macro and micro processes are gendered is not only to miss the full picture, but also, more importantly, to miss the possibilities for global justice that are evident in the work of these gendered actors.

To begin this task, I focus in this introduction on the mainstream macro perspectives on economic, political, and cultural globalizations; how they miss the contributions of the micro actors; and how gendered assumptions undergird the processes, even as they remain unacknowledged.

ECONOMIC GLOBALIZATION, OR TRADE BEYOND THE MULTINATIONAL CORPORATIONS

For most theorists of economic globalization or restructuring[1] (e.g., Bhagwati 2004; Giddens 1999; Ritzer 2004; Sklair 2002; Stiglitz 2002; Wolf 2004), the spread of neoliberal policies[2] has led to an unprecedented economic interdependency and integration resulting from global trade. Many dispute the extent of global trade. Some argue that trade is widespread and unprecedented (e.g., Sklair 2002; Robinson, 2005), while others (e.g., Hirst and Thompson 1999) argue that at the end of the nineteenth century there was more global trade, and today it is primarily among the core advanced countries. But all these theorists focus only on formal trade between countries.

The major actors who constitute formal, global trade are the multinational corporations and regulatory, intergovernmental bodies like the World Trade Organization (WTO), the World Bank, the International Monetary Fund (IMF), and regional development banks. Economists see these actors as neutral arbiters ensuring a free market for the world's capital, goods, services, and, to some extent, labor, though there are many more restrictions on labor than on goods.

Economists present this process of economic restructuring as inevitable, or, in the infamous words of the British Prime Minister Margaret Thatcher,

"There is no alternative" (TINA). Moreover, economic restructuring is desirable as it promotes economic growth and a higher, that is, "Western," standard of living for people all around the world. Since increased world trade is the answer, one would think that economists and governments who support these policies would be interested in all kinds of trade, formal and informal, that controlled by multinational corporations as well as that controlled by local people. Yet most economists seldom mention informal cross-border trade. If they do so, it is in the context of regulating it or replacing it.

Economists are silent as to who benefits from this global trade or who is involved in this trade. Feminists (e.g., Beneria 2003; Basu and Grewal 2001; Moghadam 2005) have shown that this global trade is gendered male. Men from Northern and Southern countries dominate the global trade as managers, bureaucrats, and CEOs. Even in the WTO, IMF, and World Bank, most ministers and officers are male. But educated, middle- and upper-class women, primarily in the United States and Europe and to some extent in Asia and Latin America, have also found a place in the world of formal trade, as lawyers, managers, and computer professionals (e.g., Mullings 2005). But this increase in professional women's employment hasn't led to many changes in the work culture of the professions, and it has been facilitated by the paid but devalued labor of poor women (e.g., Chang 2000; Ehrenreich and Hochschild 2002; Zimmerman, Litt, and Bose 2006).

While the managers and bureaucrats of global trade are mostly male, the global work of manufacturing and caring is mostly done by women (Fuentes and Ehrenreich 1983; Nash and Fernandez-Kelly 1983; Pyle 2006; Ward 1990; Zimmerman, Litt, and Bose 2006). Feminists have shown how the global manufacturing has become feminized in the past several decades and how women's labor-force participation has had contradictory implications for gender equality around the world (Prugl 1999; Ward 1990; Wright 2006). Feminists and economists have focused primarily on women waged workers in the global economy and the ways in which they renegotiate the patriarchal bargain. But in focusing only on women waged workers, who no doubt are the most visible aspect of the global economy, feminists too produce a narrow picture of women's work and understand women's agency as a reaction to economic global forces, emanating from outside. While in Asia and Latin America, women waged workers far outnumber women traders, in Africa the reverse is true (Pyle 2006).[3] Hence I want to highlight the role of women cross-border traders, who creatively use the openings provided by global trade to make better lives for themselves, and in so doing present other possibilities in the global era.

The world of formal, global trade is male not only in its composition but also in its assumptions and language. For example, as Joan Acker (2004, 2005) notes, gender is intrinsic to capitalist processes, as they produce structural and ideological separation between production and human re-production, with corporations bearing no responsibility for reproduction. These separations are then gendered, resulting in the masculine world of production, which is monetary, and the feminine world of reproduction, which is not monetary (Elson 1994). This ideological construction informs most managers of multinational corporations.

Male managers also make gendered assumptions about the desirability of women workers in multinational corporations (Prugl 1999; Ward 1990; Wright 2006). For example, they assume that women are docile and hence easy to control; that women have the finer motor skills and "nimble fingers" necessary for manufacturing certain high-tech products like computer chips; that women are not bored by mundane, routine assembly-line work; and that most women workers are "single" and hence can be paid less, as they are not "breadwinners," or supporters of families.

Feminists have deconstructed these assumptions over the last three decades and shown that, in reality, women workers are not docile—that they have tried to resist and organize against their working conditions and pay—and that most single women do support families, namely, parents and siblings, if not husbands and children (e.g., Beneria 2003; Basu and Grewal 2001; Fuentes and Ehrenreich 1983; Nash and Fernandez-Kelly 1983; Pyle 2006; Zimmerman, Litt, and Bose 2006). Yet such gendered constructions of the woman worker continue to inform corporate and social policies.

But such gendered understandings structure global production at its own peril, as Leslie Salzinger's (2004) analysis of Maquila workers in Mexico shows. She shows how managerial decisions are informed by gendered sense of self and others. She argues that floor managers' gendered notions of women as a docile, cheap, and readily available workforce, which they had learned in their transnational experiences in East Asia, persisted even when women became less docile and demanded higher wages and even when, by the 1980s, men were half the labor force. Rather than face this new reality, managers continued to use their gendered scripts by hiring men whom they considered more womanlike, namely, gays and transvestites. In the end, in order to meet labor needs they had to increase benefit packages to attract women, and even then there was 100 percent turnover. Thus Salzinger (2004) argues that while gendered understandings inform production processes, if managers refuse to change these expectations, they can become problematic.

In addition to the gendered assumptions regarding women workers in the global manufacturing, feminists have also shown how the academic and mainstream discourses on globalizations are themselves gendered. For example, J. K. Graham-Gibson (1996) uses the metaphor of rape to describe the discourses of globalization as a masculinist script of heteronormativity, in which globalization and rape share the language of penetration and of "virgin" markets; furthermore, the narrative of power, where violence is normalized and penetration leads to a loss, operates in both sexual and economic realms. Thus, for the developing countries, there is only one path, that of being penetrated and reshaped by "global" capital. Local is always the victim of the global (Freeman 2001). Graham-Gibson (1996) argues that "exploring ways in which the hard and penetrating body of the multinational corporations can be seen as soft, fragile, and vulnerable" can help to rethink the dominance of corporate power (147). Recognition of alternative, noncapitalist economic relations will show that capitalism is not all-encompassing.

In a similar vein, K. Chang and H. L. M. Ling (2000) demonstrate the gender of globalization by showing the two ways in which it is conceptualized, the masculine "techno-muscular" capitalism and the feminine regimes of "labor intimacy." The former includes the world of finance, production, and telecommunication, which valorizes Western capitalist masculinity masked as global, and the latter includes the manufacturing and care work done primarily by women, which is often not visible. But such an argument misses both the presence of professional women in techno-muscular capitalism and that of women at the local level who are not involved in regimes of labor intimacy, but are using the opportunities made available by global and regional openings in engaging techno-muscular capitalism.

Finally, Carla Freeman (2001) shows how globalization theories and global processes are gendered masculine even though they are assumed to be gender neutral, while ethnographic data and the local are gendered feminine. Hence, Freeman calls for an analysis of globalization that does not merely add women's stories or gendered meanings to the debate but that actually changes the way globalization is viewed, from its being seen as a larger process impacting the local to its being seen as a product of local actors' active engagement with economic restructuring. That is what I aim to do in this book.

While feminists have been showing the uneven composition and impact of global trade with respect to men and women, they too overlook women as shapers of globalization. While they show how women respond to such global trade, feminists, with few exceptions, do not see women, particularly poor women, as actors shaping globalization. This is particularly intriguing, as feminists have shown how global trade has led to an increase in women's informal labor-force participation and in women's unpaid work. So why they have missed women's informal cross-border trade is hard to understand. Perhaps they view informal cross-border trade as an extension of informal work within borders, which is often low paid, involves hard work and long hours, has no benefits, and for the most part does not help women get out of poverty. While informal cross-border trade does share some features with within-border informal trade—such as hard work, saturated markets, and low returns—it does enable women to get out of poverty, as I will show in chapter 1. But more importantly, it shows how poor women are taking advantage of economic restructuring and open borders and becoming important actors in globalization. I analyze the activities of cross-border traders in western and southern Africa and the various ways in which they present possibilities for other globalizations.

TRANSNATIONAL FEMINISTS SHAPING GLOBAL POLITICS

While most of the scholarly and popular writings on globalization tend to be about economic globalization, there has been an increase in the number of writings about political globalization since the protest against the meeting of the WTO in Seattle in 1999 (e.g., Della Porta et al. 2006; Falk 1999; Hardt and Negri 2004). Thousands of protesters from all around the world and from various movements—comprising people such as workers, farmers, environmentalists, and students, among others—gathered to protest the trade practices promoted by the WTO, which had led to the domination of TNCs in economies around the world and had increased inequalities within and between countries. The protesters took over the streets around the venue of the WTO meeting and essentially derailed it.

This protest highlighted two important aspects of what used to be called "international relations" by political scientists. First, it showed that nation-states were no longer the only, or even the major, political actors in international politics. Politics had moved beyond the borders of nation-states into the arena of supranational bodies. Supranational organizations like the WTO, the IMF, and the World Bank had become important players in international relations.

Second, the Seattle protest also revealed the importance of nonstate actors in international or global politics. Supranational bodies are often, though not always, intergovernmental bodies representing nation-states. But what Seattle revealed was the presence of protestors representing the labor movement, the environmental movement, the farmers' movements, and various other NGOs (Della Porta et al. 2006; Hardt and Negri 2004). Scholars now increasingly talk of "global civil society" (e.g., Keane 2003; Walzer 1997) to capture the politics across borders of these nonstate actors, namely movements, NGOs, and activists. But as critics of the term have noted, most of the NGOs are primarily based in Northern capitals and do not really represent the globe (e.g., Waterman 2002). Apart from not being geographically representative, NGOs also do not represent specific constituencies and hence are not accountable to anyone.

In this new global political landscape, women's movements and organizations, and women activists, have been recognized as important players (Keck and Sikkink 1998; Moghadam 2005; Naples and Desai 2002). So here the gender lens is important, not so much for seeing the presence of women's agency, as for understanding the contribution of feminist organizing in shaping a new "global politics" and in providing further possibilities for global justice movements. Researchers focusing on global politics have not seen how women's transnational organizing before the era of global politics, that is, from 1975 to 1995, has contributed to global politics in terms of developing new organizational forms such as transnational networks and new strategies based on both local and transnational organizing (e.g., Desai 2002; Ferree and Tripp 2006; Marchand and Runyan 2000; Moghadam 2005; Naples and Desai 2002; Ricciutelli, Miles, and McFadden 2004).

Women's movements and organizations have also developed new strategies of building solidarities, including what Saskia Sassen (2004) calls the "global politics of localized actors." Sassen argues that many of the transnational networks that have emerged among women's groups are very focused on local politics and issues but engage other localities on a global scale. The sites and focus of women's organizing are not global but local. Thus, women's organizing anticipated recent developments in social movement theory such as "rooted cosmopolitans," activists who are transnational but not nomadic (Tarrow 2005). Rather, they are rooted in their local communities, but also engaged with transnational politics. This is a politics that is at once space-centered and transterritorial, what Arturo Escobar (1999) calls "place-based transnational politics." This enables even resource-poor and geographically immobile actors to engage in global politics, as well as giving voice to those marginalized from formal politics at the local level.

This new global politics of localized actors is also different in that it does not have to go through nested scales from local to national to regional and international, but can be part of multiple networks that can be local-local, local-global, regional-regional, and so on. It thus represents a new local political subjectivity, framed by global realities and ideas (Sassen 2004).

Thus, a gender lens enables us to see that women's transnational activism has shaped the dominant organizational and strategic forms of contemporary global politics. Women activists are hence not just players in the global political arena, but in fact have defined the terrain of global politics. In other words, global politics is a feminist politics. This argument is the focus of chapter 2, where I show how transnational feminists, beginning with the UN Decade for Women and the Beijing Conference, have shaped global politics and how they have responded to their middle-class makeup by organizing transnational grassroots women's movements as well.

GENDER AND NEW CULTURES OF GLOBALIZATION

The debates around culture and globalization, like the debates in economic globalization, have, for the most part, been defined by globalization as a process emanating in the West. Thus globalization is seen to lead to three cultural outcomes (Nederveen Pieterse 2004): (1) homogenization of cultures around the world, or the "McDonaldization" of the world (Ritzer 1993); (2) hybridity of cultures, as people, ideas, and images from around the world intermingle and create new articulations (e.g., Appadurai 1997); (3) a clash of civilizations, or the rise of new fundamentalism, as non-Western cultures resist and resent the onslaught of Western culture (e.g., Huntington 1993).

These analysts also fall into the trap of seeing globalization as a Western force. Furthermore, most of the debates in the field have been around consumption—of food, images, music, video, films, and other cultural products. While most of these analysts do pay attention to the gendered nature of consumption in the era of global capitalism and do recognize the inequalities in these patterns, consumption still stands in for culture. I want to move away from the homogenizing, hybridity, and clash of civilization debates in the field of culture and globalization, and instead focus on the nonconsumptive, interactive cultures of globalization, in which actors are using new information and communication technologies to create new modes of communication and cultural citizenship.

Cultural citizenship has a long history in Western academic writings and was initially about bringing "high culture" to the masses (e.g., Chaney 2002; Stevenson 2003). But since the 1960s, it has been used to refer to the struggles of diverse communities, often marginalized ones, to assert the right to practice their different cultures (e.g., Kymlicka 1996). It has also been used by authoritarian governments to resist the influence of human rights dialogue and policies, particularly as they relate to women. For example, China, Malaysia, and Singapore used their "traditional" and different cultures as grounds on which to oppose certain women's rights during the UN Decade for Women (Desai 1996).

Here I want to focus on cultural citizenship as a way that communities weave their own cultural traditions and practices, along with other cultural and political traditions, via new technologies to create new cultures of globalization that are both place- and cyber-based, and which enable women to communicate with local, national, and transnational communities working around gender justice. I use the concept of hybridity to demonstrate hybridity of meaning making.

My conception of new cultures of globalization is similar to Nederveen Pieterse's articulation of transnational culture, a product of "transnational influence and cooperation in technology, media, popular culture, art, functional domains and professions" (Nederveen Pieterse 2007, 204). But we differ in that his transnational culture is an instrumental and functional product of transnational flows, while I emphasize the process that leads to new meanings that borrow from multiple cultures, or what Nederveen

Pieterse has called "flexible acculturation," the reality of actors traversing and borrowing from multiple circuits of identity and symbols. As actors encounter multiple cultures, they move back and forth between them.

I combine flexible acculturation with cultural citizenship to show how men and women are creating alternative circuits of cultural vocabulary and affiliation. While most of Nederveen Pieterse's examples are of marginal groups in the West who engage in flexible acculturation around religion and music, I focus on how both marginal and mainstream people use flexible acculturation to create alternative circuits, with the aim of claiming cultural citizenship.

Cultural citizenship via new cultures of globalization is the focus of chapter 3, where I show how Independent Media Centers and Women's Programming Support Networks are examples of how men and women are creating new cultures based on their realities and global openings, and in so doing are shaping globalization around the world as much as the television programs, films, and music videos are.

POLITICS OF POSSIBILITIES

The aim of my analysis is to show how and why a gender lens is invaluable to rethinking globalizations, and thus to contributing to a critical globalization studies as well as to possibilities for global justice movements. William I. Robinson (2005) defines *critical globalization studies* as a field that produces analyses that challenge the mainstream understanding of globalizations, as well as one that attempts to link theory to practice. By focusing on how women and men in specific economic, political, and cultural arenas are shaping globalizations, I offer possibilities for both critical globalization studies and the global justice movements.

By "possibilities," I mean both what is possible given the current structural realities in which we find ourselves, as well as what can be possible based on our collective imagination and creativity. The agency of women in the next three chapters reveals many examples of both of these possibilities.

NOTES

1. Following Marchand (2003), I use the term *economic restructuring* as opposed to *economic globalization*, as it is a process that is still underway and not yet complete.

2. *Neoliberal* policies, also often referred to as the Washington Consensus, are a set of economic policies that highlight privatization of all production and services,

the opening of domestic markets to TNCs, and the orienting of domestic economic production toward export. In the context of the Global South, these neoliberal policies have been translated into structural adjustment programs.

3. This asymmetry reflects the role of Asia and the U.S.-Mexican border as the test cases for the global assembly line. Latin America, due to its proximity to the United States, has also provided a lot of care workers.

1

Women Cross-Border Traders[1]

The New Cosmopolitans of Globalization

> Stand at any of South Africa's border posts and watch who is crossing the border to neighboring states. Women with heads and arms laden, bakkies and cars overloaded with goods, mini-bus taxis pulling trailers, and lorries—big and small filled to the brim. Trains and buses pull in with full baggage racks. Many of these vehicles are carrying informal sector cross-border traders, people who are better described as small entrepreneurs involved in importing and exporting, or trading, across one or more of the borders in the region. They are carrying goods ranging from fruit and vegetables to mattresses, stereos, duvets and other household goods. Traveling into South Africa, vehicles and hands are often empty—but not always. Refrigerated trucks and bakkies carry fish and shellfish. Other cars, buses, trains and pedestrians carry handicrafts and curios, wire, crochet work, traditional dresses, capulanas, coal and vegetables. (Peberdy 2002, 35)

What Peberdy describes at South African border crossings is a phenomenon that has become increasingly familiar at border crossings across the world. Women constitute between 60 and 70 percent of cross-border traders,[2] and their trade constitutes between 20 and 30 percent of all cross-border trade (e.g., Chen 2001; CORN and AFSC 2004a; Morris and Saul 2005; Murshid and Sokphally 2005).

Yet most economists and analysts of global trade focus primarily on trade by TNCs that cross borders without restraints (e.g., Beneria 2003; Castells 1999; Sklair 2002; Sassen 2006). Analysts studying corporate global trade focus on the volume of trade, the balance of trade between countries, how most of the trade is among subsidiaries of the same TNCs, and how trade is good for economic growth. In such an analysis of global trade, actors, particularly women, become invisible. The only visible actors, besides the

TNCs, are the primarily male managers, investment bankers, and corporate CEOs who move huge sums of money and goods across borders.

If women appear in this picture, it is as low-paid, exploited workers producing the goods; as caregivers providing for the managers' families; and as microcredit[3] recipients who are responsible economic agents. Even in feminist analyses of gender and globalization, women appear mostly as exploited workers and transnational caregivers (e.g., Beneria 2003; Zimmerman, Litt, and Bose 2006). But economic restructuring has also provided openings for women cross-border traders. To develop a more nuanced understanding of the relationship of gender to processes of economic globalization, we need to chart the trajectories of these women as well.

Another common assumption of scholars studying economic globalization is that globalization has bypassed Africa. African women are seen as being victims of structural adjustment without benefiting from globalization. Even feminist scholarship on globalization and gender, including my own, has seen African women as involved in globalization processes primarily through their agricultural labor, work in the "informal" economy, and unpaid labor in the house. Like many scholars, I had failed to see how African women were in fact shaping processes of the global economy.

This failing on our part is a result of understanding processes of economic globalizations (1) only in terms of the industrial sector and corporate trade and (2) as proceeding in a linear fashion, emanating in the West. This linear vision of economic globalization persisted even as we saw cultural and political globalization processes as part of multidirectional flows. It was only as I began to question this dominant understanding of economic globalization that I was able to see how African women were in fact shaping economic globalization processes, albeit not to the same extent and in the same way as TNCs. But they were more than just victims of structural adjustment policies.

This rethinking was also motivated by my changing understanding of women's agency. Feminist formulation of women's agency is often reactive, that is, it is formulated as a response to patriarchal practices. Within this framework, women either resist or reproduce social norms through their actions (e.g., Butler 1999). I want to work from a creative or constructive formulation of women's agency, where women are not just reacting or responding to patriarchal circumstances but creatively fashioning a way in the world. In so doing, they draw upon multiple resources that have multiple consequences.[4]

In this chapter, I want to address this invisibility of African women's agency in processes of global economic restructuring by showing how some women in southern and western Africa, drawing on their "traditional" market role in many societies, have benefited from the global openings to engage in and shape global processes at the local and regional levels. As 30 percent of households in Africa are headed by women, this form of economic activity is important not only to their households but also to their regional and national economies (Morris and Saul 2005).

Recently, women's cross-border trade has received attention from donors such as the U.S. Agency for International Development and the World Bank as an avenue for reducing poverty and increasing food security (e.g., Murshid and Sokphally 2005; CORN and AFSC 2004a; Carr and Chen 2002). What this instrumental analysis of women's cross-border trade misses, however, is the opportunity to reconceive economic globalization and the possibilities that such a reconception offers. I fear that a unidimensional analysis of cross-border trade, as a strategy for poverty reduction, will have the same fate as microcredit. It will become a panacea for problems relating to women's lack of economic and social empowerment and will be hijacked by neoliberal rhetoric and programs of NGOs and the UN system.

As a caution against such a reductionist possibility, I offer an analysis of women cross-border traders as innovators and important global actors responding to structural adjustment programs and global economic restructuring. As such, they encounter, like other global actors, structural constraints and opportunities that have implications for political economies, social identities, and social justice.

I focus on how some poor women have used global economic openings to become cross-border traders. In the process, they have developed regional socioeconomic networks that have enabled them to raise their standard of living. Most women cross-border traders are able to build new houses, provide education for their children as public education becomes scarce, and expand their business. Cross-border trade has also enabled women to become independent, to articulate a new collective identity, and to develop local and regional economies based on creative responses to the uncertainties created by the structural adjustment programs in the region.

Cross-border trading is not restricted to poor women. In many West and North African countries, middle- and upper-class women also engage in cross-border trade and bring in foreign consumer items for men and women in local markets. In southern Africa, cross-border trade was made possible by the new immigration policies of the postapartheid regime, which enabled other Africans to travel freely to South Africa, as well as by the structural adjustment programs that created the need for women to become traders.

I will examine both middle-class and poor women traders to show how women constitute globalization even as they are impacted by it. In their lived experience and history they are defining a new cosmopolitanism, different from that described in the theoretical reflections of Western academics and from that of global corporations trying to spread cosmopolitan consumption. It is what Jan Nederveen Pieterse (2006) calls an "emancipatory cosmopolitanism," which is not based on preconceived norms but emerges from women's lived experience and action.

I begin, however, with a review of analyses of women in local, "informal" economies and globalization, to inform my analysis of cross-border trade in western and southern Africa, and I conclude with a discussion of how my analysis presents us with another perspective on economic globalization processes that highlights the agency of ordinary women.

WOMEN IN LOCAL ECONOMIES

In the early 1970s, Third World feminists and labor activists began noting the rise of women's paid economic activities in the so-called "informal" sectors in the urban centers of the developing world. Economists and urban sociologists analyzed it as a consequence of modernization and development. The International Labour Organization defined it as work that is "pre-modern"; that exists alongside the modern, industrial, or formal economy; and that is marked by low income, low capital, low skills, and unstable employment (International Labour Organization 1972). Furthermore, such work involves unregulated hours and conditions of work, insecurity, and no taxation. Thus, workers tend to be poor and lack social protection, although they contribute to economic growth. This sector is very heterogeneous and includes street vendors, domestic workers, and home-based workers. Carr and Chen 2002 classify informal workers into three categories: employers, self-employed, and casual wage labor.

In Latin America, such employment accounts for 55 percent of the population; in Asia, between 45 and 85 percent; and in Africa, about 80 percent (Women in Informal Employment: Globalizing and Organizing 2001). This "informal" work comprises 50–80 percent of all nonagricultural employment and contributes 20–65 percent to the gross domestic product (GDP). In Africa, depending on the country, it provides employment to 18–74 percent of the population, and women constitute around 65 percent of such economic activity. Most of these women are heads of households. Furthermore, this economic activity contributes between 30 and 50 percent of GDP in sub-Saharan Africa (Akinboade 2005).

At the national level, this economy is made up of home-based workers as well as street workers. Home-based workers include those who use household labor to run a small enterprise and those workers who do piecework under subcontract with formal operations. In Africa, more women tend to be self-employed and work in family-owned businesses than work as casual labor (Akinboade 2005). Yet most of this women's paid work is not counted. Now, decades after feminists struggled to count women's unpaid work, the struggle is to count women's paid work that remains invisible.

Economists explain the presence of the "informal" sector in three ways: *dualism*, *structuralism*, and *legalism* (Carr and Chen 2002). The dualists differentiate between the formal and "informal" sectors and assume that there are no relations between the two. The "informal" sector is seen as a parallel or underground economy. Structuralists (e.g., Castells and Portes 1989) see the "informal" sector as having vertical ties to the formal sector and, in fact, subsidizing it through low wages. The legalists see the "informal" economy as a rational choice by entrepreneurs who are constrained by too many regulations.

Thus, it is the understanding of power relations that differentiates the three explanations (Carr and Chen 2002). The dualists see people in the "informal" economy as having no power, while the legalists see people as exercising their power to make a different choice, and structuralists see "informal" workers as having little power as they negotiate between the two sectors. As I show in this chapter, based on the experiences of cross-border traders in Africa, women do have power to make choices, even though those choices are constrained by the local and global economies.

Most economists predicted that as economies became more industrialized and hence developed, the "informal" sector would decline. They expected economic growth in the industrial sector to absorb most workers. On the contrary, in the era of globalization the "informal" economy has grown in most parts of the world, including in Europe and North America (Women in Informal Employment: Globalizing and Organizing 2001). Part of the reason for the increase, rather than decrease, of the "informal" economy has to do with the kind of economic growth that occurs under globalization. Most of it has been capital-intensive growth or jobless growth that has not provided employment but instead forced people to resort to the "informal" economy.

The global economy is also fueled by high-technology services that require professional education. This excludes a majority of people around the world, especially women, who thus turn to the "informal" economy. At the same time, export-oriented trade policies of economic restructuring also expand this economy, as there is demand in the export market for products such as handicrafts, textiles, and other local goods, primarily produced in this economy. Finally, in times of economic restructuring and crisis we see a rise in the "informal" economy, as more and more people find themselves outside the wage sector (Carr and Chen 2002).

Depending on the segment of the "informal" economy in which one works, the impacts of economic restructuring vary. For example, restructuring has benefited those women who are self-employed and own small businesses or enterprises, as they can now link to the global commodity chains and have access to global markets. Women who are cross-border traders have, for the most part, benefited from restructuring. Most cross-border traders sell goods produced in the world market, thus benefiting either TNCs or other manufacturers in other parts of the world. If there were efforts to enable cross-border traders to sell goods produced regionally, it would further benefit regional and local trade.

Another impact of economic restructuring, according to S. Marjit and D. S. Maiti (2005), is an increase in wages in the "informal" sector. But because this wage increase occurs along with high unemployment, there are more people crowding into the "informal" economy. This leads to what economists call the "crowding out" effect, where small firms and entrepreneurs are crowded out by larger, and often foreign, firms, even in the "informal" economy.

While most analyses of the "informal" economy have focused on the "informal" economy within nation-states, there have been a few studies on cross-border trade as well. Yahya Hashim and Kate Meaghar (1999) argue that the theoretical perspectives on cross-border trade fall into five categories. First, the neoliberal, market-led economic view sees evidence of cross-border trade as an indication that state regulations do not work and that there is thus need for greater deregulation. Those favoring this perspective see cross-border trade as regional integration from below.

The historical and empirical perspectives (also often within a neoliberal framework) emphasize the history, the organization of cross-border trade along ethnic and long-distance networks, the commodities traded, and how the networks are used. Another economic perspective sees it as a parallel economy that is free from state regulation and more authentically "bourgeois," one that is also a fertile ground for civil society organizations.

These studies show that not everyone benefits from cross-border trade, particularly when one looks at the experiences of women, and that most of the ethnic networks of trade tend to be authoritarian. The final perspective emphasizes how cross-border trade is an indication of how fragile and futile borders are in containing economic activity and social organizations. These authors argue that economic restructuring can lead to alternative social organizations beyond ethnic and other ties.

I agree with the analysts who emphasize the importance of networks in cross-border trade. I, however, see women cross-border traders as innovators using new economic opportunities and thus participating in economic restructuring. As I show below, women often create their own networks and do not rely only on ethnic or other kin networks. Finally, I see cross-border trade as enabling women to create empowering identities and to engage in a politics of possibilities.

WOMEN IN THE GLOBAL ECONOMY: CROSS-BORDER TRADE IN SOUTHERN AND WESTERN AFRICA[5]

I [Tebogo Serurubele] went to South Africa to buy small packets of second-hand clothes to sell. After making some profit, I included new items in my business such as clothes, decorating vases, comforters, and started going to Zambia to buy bales of second-hand clothes. I am still doing this now.

My destination to sell my commodities is the capital city, Gaborone, and surrounding villages but in future I intend to go further inland to the villages. So far, there is no business there. I also sell in the flea market. I trade daily, although many times I come back home empty-handed. (CORN and AFSC 2004d)

Sisi is [a] forty-five year old Ghanaian woman who engages in what has become known as the Accra-London-Accra business. . . . This new group of enterprising women has now extended its purchasing destinations beyond the West African sub-region to London, New York and, in recent years, to Asian cities such as Bangkok and Hong Kong. They buy a variety of consumer goods . . . which they resell in Ghana for profit. (Darkwah 2007, 64–65)

These two narratives provide an idea of what cross-border trade involves. The volume of cross-border trade in Africa varies from $7 million to $177 million. In most parts it is primarily responsible for food security, as neither the state nor the markets provide this for a majority of the people.

Like the "informal" economy at the national level, cross-border trade is defined by low cash flows, small consignments, no taxation, and traders accompanying their consignments. Following the introduction of structural adjustment programs in Southern African Development Community countries in the 1980s and 1990s, a third of the population lived in poverty and 70 percent were unemployed. Many turned to cross-border trade for survival.

However, not all cross-border trade is a response solely to global economic restructuring. Historically, in many African countries, particularly in West Africa, trading was a women's activity. This was further facilitated under colonialism, when men became wage earners and women augmented their agricultural activity with trade. Women, in essence, formed their own social economies.

Most cross-border trade in Africa is gendered in terms of kinds of goods traded, the volume traded, access to capital, kind of transportation used, and location of business. Gender inequality in most countries limits women's access to credit, transportation, and mobility. As a result, women tend to concentrate in low-profit, highly competitive trade in agricultural and food products and services. They often sell directly on the streets or in markets, and they rarely use a vehicle or own their own vehicles.

Men, by contrast, tend to concentrate in value-added goods such as car parts, nonedible products, and consumer goods. Often they are wholesalers, have shops, or sell to larger retail outlets; and they often use and own their own vehicles, such as bicycles, trucks, or minibuses (e.g. Macamo 1999; Minde and Nakhumwa 1998).

Like Tebogo and Sisi, most women in western and southern Africa began cross-border trade in the 1990s as a result of structural adjustment policies.

Most are widows, divorcees, or single women in the 20–47 age range. They had moved to urban areas after independence, as colonial policies prevented women from being in urban areas before then. Women traders support anywhere from 4 to 7 dependents. Since 1995, more men have been engaging in cross-border trade, as they see in it opportunities for making profit. The impact of men entering this field has not been studied widely.

The goods women trade in either direction vary. Some tend to specialize in particular products. For example, women from southern Zimbabwe bring crocheted and knitted clothing into South Africa. Most traders, however, avoid concentrating on particular goods, as a hedge against market fluctuations.

The cross-border economy is diverse and consists of many different kinds of traders. In southern Africa, analysts have differentiated traders based on the duration of their stay in the foreign country. Thus, Sally Peberdy (2002) distinguishes between *shoppers*—women who travel to South Africa for one to four days to buy goods from wholesale outlets to sell in their own countries—and *traders*—women who travel, for example, for a week to two months, sometimes across several countries.

In western Africa, analysts have differentiated cross-border trade by the scale of trading. For example, based on a study in Mali, Senegal, Benin, Ghana, Burkina Faso, Côte d'Ivoire, and Nigeria, Gayle Morris and Mahir Saul (2005) define three categories of traders: *retailer*, *wholesaler/retailer*, and *wholesaler*. The retailers usually buy and sell in local markets, do not travel very far, and usually sell "fancy" cloth and enamel cookware, and goods of lower value and volume.

Wholesaler/retailers buy wholesale, sell retail and/or wholesale, buy and travel in regional markets, and sell in local and regional markets. They tend to have higher-value items such as "real" cloth, plastics, aluminum cook sets, and Abidjan cosmetics, and they also have a higher volume of trade.

The wholesalers buy and sell wholesale exclusively, diversify into other activities and product lines, and travel to regional and cross-regional markets, particularly Dubai. They sell goods like Austrian cloth, Turkish glassware, Dubai kitchen products, and European cosmetics. They have the highest volume and value of goods and also make the most profit. The other categories of traders often end up in saturated markets with low profits. So to retain a competitive edge, traders are secretive about their supply sources and are constantly on the lookout for either new products or new markets.

Elite women traders travel to global cities in Europe, the United States, Asia, Latin America, and the Middle East. On average, they spend between $5,000 and $10,000 on each transnational trip (Darkwah 2007). They sell hair-care products, beauty products, clothes, shoes, bags, belts, kitchen equipment, and electronics. Most elite traders own shops and had mothers who were traders. The consumers of most cross-border goods are also women. Men, however, are the primary consumers for car parts and used cars.

Poor women in western and southern Africa face similar barriers, such as lack of credit and other services, lack of information about ways to increase profitability, poor transportation, complicated customs forms and procedures, poor security, and limited information about international and regional markets (Morris and Saul 2005). Because women do not have access to commercial credit, most do business in cash, and so carry large amounts, which puts them at risk. In addition, women also face harassment from border guards and customs officers.

To respond to all these situations, as I show below, women cross-border traders in western and southern Africa develop varied kin and nonkin networks. In the process, they also articulate new collective identities.

Social Networks of Cross-Border Trade in Western and Southern Africa

The following narrative provides a description of what is involved in cross-border trade for poor women, who are the majority of cross-border traders:

I [Tebogo Serurubele] became a trader because . . . As a single parent and breadwinner, I realized that my salary was not sufficient to cover the cost of my rent, food, transport and clothes for my children. This was the economic situation that forced me to become a cross-border trader, to try and increase my income.

I use public transport when I go to the Republic of South Africa or to Zambia and when I arrive I have to use taxis to ferry my goods from shop to shop and to the bus terminus. We even have to pay the loaders. Sometimes the journey to our destination is uncomfortable as there will be many people all traveling with luggage. This makes it very difficult to move when you want to go out. Here at home I use my vehicle. Accommodation outside the country is not easy.

I sleep in cheap guesthouses and hotels in shared rooming, which is only what I can afford. Even at home when I trade, I do not have any shelter where I can sit and sell. So I just sit in the centre of the mall using my umbrella for cover. If it rains, I stay home. If it is windy, then it is a problem. It is hard to find a market for our goods because we are many and are selling the same commodities. Hence the income I get from trading is not much.

In the mall where we sell there are no public toilets. I really wonder what the planners concerned were thinking about? Why did they not just provide the facilities and we could pay? Across the border generally the sanitation is very bad. Toilets are extremely dirty which is very unhygienic.

In some countries, like Zambia, in private properties like shops or restaurants where the bus stops to let us buy some food to eat, we pay for the toilets. At the bus terminus we pay K (kwacha[6])1000 for the toilets but they are not properly looked after—water on the floor. At others we pay K2000 to bath [sic] there. There is no courtesy at the borders. Most of the officers when talking to you they look at you as if we are not normal. Sometimes you feel bad about them. They are supposed to treat even people who have done wrong politely. So far, I cannot see any long-term benefits in this business as we only exist from hand to mouth. There is nowhere to get finance to boost our trade, as financial institutions do not want to sponsor the informal traders. (CORN and AFSC 2004d)

For poor women like Tebogo, cross-border trade represents a way to earn a livelihood and address the inequalities created by the structural adjustment policies. Cross-border travel is regional, hard, arduous, and open to many risks, including that of harassment. For middle-class women, cross-border trade represents upward mobility and profits. Travel is more global and not as hard. Both groups of women, however, rely on social networks of kin and nonkin to transact their border crossings.

Women traders develop two kinds of social networks: trading networks and social-support networks that facilitate their ability to do business. Both kinds of networks include kin and nonkin. The nonkin networks are a result of women's own initiative. Over time, women tend to move away from kin networks, as kin tend to be more demanding than nonkin. Traders have more control over the reciprocal relationships with nonkin, where they pay in kind in terms of food and other goods from their trade (Muzvidziwa 2001).

The trading networks, in turn, are of three kinds: one for entry into the trade and getting credit; a second for transportation and border crossing; and the third for developing and maintaining a client base. Most traders are initiated into cross-border trade by a friend or a relative. Women move from local, retail trade to wholesale regional trade as they make more connections and increase their scale of trade. They then reduce it as they age and transfer their trade to their kin. Thus women move in a "trading career"—from selling, in local markets, goods bought by older women in faraway markets to becoming long-distance traders themselves (Morris and Saul 2005).

Women become involved with other traders and trade associations to move on to the ultimate objective, which is to travel to Dubai or Hong Kong to purchase higher-end electronic and household goods, as well as cosmetics. The trajectory of cross-border trader from one category to another depends on whether she is rural or urban, her level of literacy, and her network connections. Clearly, the further afield you trade, the more you are likely to succeed economically.

Once women decide to trade, getting capital is their major concern. Most poor women generate capital through governmental or nongovernmental credit societies.

I had no capital to start with, so I went to the Women's Finance House (Emang Basadi) to ask for help. I was told to look for four other people to make a group, give it a name, elect office bearers and choose the Chairperson. I did as I was asked to do and I was elected as the Chairperson of the group called Polokano. We were given a loan of P (pula[7]) 2500.00. After repaying it, we were given another loan of P3500.00. It was then that the problems started. Some of the members could not pay and we were expected to repay our loans with interest. The group broke up but, from my small savings, I managed to continue my business. (CORN and AFSC 2004d)

Most poor women borrow money from *marounds* (rotation clubs) for their business. Elite women often start their businesses with gifts of capital, of about $4,000, from their mothers. The elite women are known as *business-women*, not *traders*; their shops are registered, and they pay taxes. They have local and foreign bank accounts and have between $5,000 and $20,000 in working capital (Darkwah 2007). They also command social respect for their entrepreneurial skills and the service they provide to consumers in their countries.

Transportation and the ability to process paperwork are crucial aspects of cross-border trade. Almost all relationships related to these two aspects of trade are mediated by men. Hence, among the trade networks that women develop are those with men. These men are transporters, freight forwarders, and money changers (Morris and Saul 2005). *Transporters* are intermediaries who connect women with men who own vehicles they can use. Sometimes transporters also extend credit to women who don't have enough capital and act as buying agents for them. The *freight forwarders* are men who get the customs documentation and clearance, as each country has different requirements. They include in their fees bribes for the various customs officials and other roadblocks, which can range from $2 to $70. Most women see this as the price of doing business and are not outraged by it.

The formation of the Economic Community of West African States, the West African Economic and Monetary Union, and the Southern African Development Community was, in each case, meant to promote free trade in the region, to give preferential treatment for goods manufactured in the region, to lower tariffs and other barriers, and to standardize documents and procedures in order to simplify the paperwork. These regional trade agreements still have not been implemented fully, and, where they have, women do not know of these new policies. In West Africa, most local and government officials are pro-trader, as most have sisters, mothers, or wives who are involved in trade (Morris and Saul 2005).

The government and businesses in Dubai, a popular destination of Francophone traders, are taking on the provision of some of these services, such as having French translators, currency brokers, storage facilities, and freight forwarders who organize the transportation of women's goods back home. Dubai then becomes the beginning of further transnational trade from Southeast Asia and South Asia. Women who travel to Dubai and further afield spend anywhere from $10,000 to $75,000 a trip (Morris and Saul 2005).

Finally, success depends on a base of loyal customers who will buy from the women on a regular basis. Hence, women have to develop and maintain client networks. But the vagaries of economic globalization mean that the prices of their goods fluctuate. At the same time, the decline of public subsidies for food, housing, and education has diminished the purchasing power of the majority of the people. Thus, the consumer items that elite women sell have become harder to buy. The elite businesswomen promote the consumption of Western goods by exhorting their clients to buy a few good things that are made in the West as opposed to many cheap goods made locally, promoting the consumption of Western goods over local ones. Consumption of Western goods also accrues social status for the consumers. Hence, middle- and upper-class women buy from the elite traders despite the difficulty of affording those goods.

In southern Africa, women develop and maintain two sets of client networks: one in the home country, for the goods acquired in the foreign country, and the other in the foreign country, to sell goods from the home country. Such dual networks are not as prevalent in West Africa, where women primarily bring goods to sell in their home countries. They rarely take goods from their home countries to sell in the foreign countries.

In addition to the trade networks analyzed above, women also need social support to enable them to carry on their trade. They need inexpensive places to live and to store their goods, and kin to look after their children and family while they travel to buy and sell goods.

> Having her husband in New York City provided Sisi with a home in the developed world to which she could return when on a purchasing trip. Not having to spend money on hotel bills meant that Sisi had more capital at her disposal on each purchasing trip. Sisi would usually travel twice a year for a period of two weeks each to purchase her items. While she was away in New York City purchasing more items for her shop, her father, a retired civil servant, supervised her shop. For the rest of the year, Sisi would stay put in her shop overseeing the day to day operations of the shop. (Darkwah 2007, 64–65)

Like Sisi, most women traders depend on family members or nonkin helpers to look after their families while they travel. Many are part of all-female households (Muzvidziwa 2001). Hence some of them take on male boarders to ensure the security of their families while they are gone.

In addition to actively creating and reproducing kin and nonkin networks to initiate them into the business, provide credit and a client base, enable travel and accommodation during buying and selling expeditions, and support their families in their absence, women traders also articulate new collective identities, as I show below.

Vakadzi Veku Sout (Women of the South): New Cosmopolitan and Other Social Identities

Most cross-border traders are primarily urban women between the ages of 15 and 47 who are better educated than men of the same age group in their countries. For example, studies conducted in various African countries found that 90 percent of the traders were educated, with 40 percent having some formal qualification such as a secondary-school certificate or other training certificate, and 9 percent even having some university experience (Cheater 1998; Muzvidziwa 2001). The high proportion of educated traders reflects both a lack of employment in many western and southern African countries and the desire of educated people to travel and create their own livelihood.

Most women traders are married, divorced, or widowed, and often they are heads of households (e.g., Dodson 1998; Muzvidziwa 2001). As a result, most traders identify as both mothers and heads of households, responsible for the well-being of their families. Young, never-married women rarely engage in cross-border trade. This could reflect the greater immobility of single women due to patriarchal and other constraints, as well as the greater need of married women to support their families.

Cross-border trading has enabled women not only to fulfill their responsibilities as mothers and heads of households, but also to develop other economic and social identities, such as those of trader/businesswoman and cosmopolitan. As Peberdy and Jonathan Crush (1998) found, many see themselves as entrepreneurs and do not seek formal employment. Many enjoy trade, and some even see themselves as artists and artisans.

Women traders' desire for self-employment not only highlights the agency of women but also reveals the creativity and enterprising spirit of people. Often the livelihood strategies of poor men and women are labeled as survival or coping strategies rather than creative or innovative ways of addressing the situations in which they find themselves. Creativity is an important human desire that we all share and express in different ways given the constraints of our situation.

In addition to developing new identities, cross-border traders are also undermining old gender patterns of migration, particularly in southern Africa. Women who migrate across borders challenge the historical, geographic, and temporal patterns of apartheid-era migration (Cheater 1998; Cheater and Gaidzanwa 1996). The historical pattern was primarily male, with men going to seek formal employment in apartheid-era mining, agricultural, and other industries located in industrial townships. While this male migration was impermanent, as the apartheid regime wanted to secure low-wage workers without giving them any security of permanent residence, it was long-term. By contrast, cross-border traders are primarily women, who go not for formal employment but for trade. Hence they tend to go to larger urban towns and cities. Moreover, their visits are short-term and the movement is back and forth across borders, or *transmigration*.

The responses to the success and mobility of women traders are very different in western Africa from those in South Africa. In West Africa they are hailed as successful women who are contributing to their national economies. In South Africa, women traders are labeled and stigmatized, especially by middle-class South Africans, journalists, police officers, and other government officials (McDonald et al. 1998). They see women traders as "migrants" coming to use social services, bringing crime and disease, and causing the fiscal instability of the economy. It is striking how the discourse against migrants in South Africa is similar to the discourse against undocumented Latinos in the United States, despite the distance and difference between the two contexts.

Despite such stigmatization, cross-border traders come to South Africa for visits with family, to trade, to shop, and, in some cases, to work. Most do not want to live in South Africa; despite the better services, low cost of living, and employment opportunities, they prefer to live in their own countries, where they have access to land, water, family, and community. Most of the traders, particularly those engaged in selling curios and handicrafts to tourists, come to South Africa because it is the biggest tourist destination for both African and Western tourists and has the best economy on the continent. Hence, it offers more opportunities for trade.

The stigmatization of cross-border traders also reveals gender anxieties (e.g., Cheater 1998; Dodson 1998; Muzvidziwa 2001). The terms that have been used to describe traders are similar to terms used in other cultures at other times to question and denounce women's agency. Most commonly, women traders are accused of being "witches." They are seen as engaging in ritual murder and carrying on a cross-border trade in body parts for ritual medicines, or *muti*.

Another common response to women traders is to attack their sexuality. The range of attacks displays both fear of working women and hostility toward them. Traders are accused of being prostitutes, servicing the truckers they encounter in their border crossings; they are stigmatized as victims of rape; or they are thought to spread HIV/AIDS. This last attack is particularly potent, as in the context of the HIV/AIDS epidemic in southern Africa, trade in muti, traditional medicines, and biological resources has increased and comprises almost $700 million (Akinboade 2005).

Some reports also see women's cross-border trade as expeditions to seek abortions. In Zimbabwe, press reports accuse them of everything from being "unpatriotic" to being "volatile women," "smugglers," and "abortion organizers" (Cheater 1998). Clearly, cross-border travel of independent women is seen as threatening on a number of levels. Most importantly, they challenge both the state's and communities' patriarchal authority, formal and informal, including the power to grant citizenship. As Angela Cheater (1998) notes:

> These women survive well financially, dealing in hi-tech goods with uses that baffle men. They develop business relations with wealthy and more powerful consumers. They shrug off the dangers of rape in developing board and accommodation networks in foreign lands with previously unknown distant and classificatory kin and unrelated strangers. They use state entitlements against all expectations. They know their way around complex state and banking bureaucracies, without the benefit of high levels of formal education or personal relations of (male) patronage. (208)

In short, they act as cosmopolitans, hold passports, and travel between countries. The raids against them, for example in the central business districts of both Johannesburg and Cape Town, haven't prevented them from continuing to engage in the risky business of cross-border trade, even though such raids have cost them a great deal economically as well as socially, stigmatizing them even further (Peberdy and Crush 1998).

In addition to assaults on their sexuality, women traders are also criticized for their economic activities. They are seen as illegal actors engaging in smuggling, when in fact most women are engaged in legal trade. Similar accusations are not leveled against men who engage in cross-border trade. Women traders are also viewed as unpatriotic economic agents, as they use up much-needed foreign currency in their trade. Such economic criticisms fail to recognize that many women traders engage local women in their home countries to make items for trade, thus providing livelihood to other women besides themselves, and also employ women in the foreign countries.

Almost 20 percent of cross-border traders in South Africa hire local South African men and women to help them out, and also to purchase a lot of goods produced in South Africa, to be traded back home. Most traders spend 40–50 percent of their earnings in South Africa. Hence, they benefit the South African economy in numerous ways. In South Africa, however, cross-border traders are seen as competition, undercutting local women trading in the "informal" sector.

The response to women traders highlights the double standards of South Africa's trade policy (e.g., Cheater 1998; Peberdy and Crush 1998). The official policy of South Africa is to expand exports and to have access to the markets of other African countries. Since the 1990s, over 30 percent of South Africa's foreign direct investments are in other African markets all over the continent. So the South African government wants open borders for its businesses, but does not want to open its borders to other southern African traders.

Despite the attack on their identities as traders, women cross-border traders are creative social agents. They are postcolonial subjects with multiple identities, who invoke and use different identities in conjunction with economic strategies as well as interpersonal relationships (Muzvidziwa 2001). For example, they use the "witch" label to their advantage to ensure debt collection from clients who default or do not pay on time. They also use being black in South Africa, or being a "Rhodie" for their white clients in South Africa (where many white "Rhodesians" settled after Zimbabwe became independent).

At the border, they deal with the patriarchal state that denies them legitimate access by bribing officials when necessary and challenging them at other times. They know that their political and economic citizenships often do not coincide, and they are not afraid to live with that contradiction. Hence, they are also known as *svejks*, people who undermine the state from within.

Another way in which women in southern Africa identify themselves is as *Vakadzi Veku Sout*, women of the South (Muzvidziwa 2001). These are poor women who recognize and use multiple identities to form alliances and networks of support across borders. Cross-border traders exhibit a culture that transcends both nationality and ethnicity and is based on attitudes, values, and behavior that Cheater (1998) calls "corporate culture" in the "informal" sector. They have a unique style of dressing; but, more importantly, they have a way of being in the world, and values that cross ethnic differences.

While southern African women espouse a cosmopolitan identity across borders, women in West Africa have a different identity. The Shabe traders who live along the Nigeria/Benin border have shaped border identities that are neither hybrid nor nationless—that is, they are neither displaced nor deterritorial, but rather their identity is based on deep rootedness in the border region (Flynn 1997). Thus, although divided by national borders, people living on either side of the border share a close bond, as depicted in this common song sung in the region: "The Okpara river from which we drink, you also drink from it; so we are brothers and sisters and we are together" (Flynn 1997, 311).

Border residents use their border identity for both economic and political power by collecting taxes from nonlocals. The taxes are then used for collective purposes. Border residents also act as intermediaries between the local and nonlocal traders who cross their borders. Border residents are deeply aware of their national borders and identities, as it is the border identities that enable them to engage in their economic activities. Without a border there would be no tolls to collect. This border identity is based on length of residence rather than ethnicity or gender. Hence it is a place-based identity. And yet it is developed in opposition to the state, represented by the border guards and customs officials whom border residents challenge continuously as they collect their own taxes from cross-border traders.

Most work on cosmopolitanism has dealt with middle- and upper-class cosmopolitans, either in the North or the South (e.g., Archibugi 2003; Cheah and Robbins 1998; Ong 1999). But it is becoming common in many border areas of the world, where state and citizenship requirements are being breached daily in creative ways by poor women, for trade as well as for solidarity. Women cross-border traders have cut across ethnic differences in helping each other make the most of the economic opportunities. Hence, poor women are undermining ethnic differences across the state borders and within them and demonstrating another way to be cosmopolitan, what Nederveen Pieterse (2006) calls "emancipatory cosmopolitanism." It derives from their lived experience of cross-border trade, rather than a normative or theoretical consideration. Women cross-border traders' cosmopolitanism is not about hybrid identities, as their identities continue to be embedded in specific milieus, but it is about action. Hence for the *Vakadzi Veku Sout*, trade is not just a refuge from unemployment, but a way of being in the world. And it is from these locations that they articulate alternatives that can enable us to formulate other possibilities, as I will discuss in the last chapter.

Rethinking Economic Globalization

In this chapter I have examined economic globalization in terms of women's cross-border trade as opposed to corporate trade, which is the focus of the mainstream literature on economic globalization. I have done this for several reasons. First, this trade is more important to the livelihoods of most women and men around the world than corporate cross-border trade. Second, corporate trade emphasizes the role of disembodied actors such as TNCs and multilateral institutions and is silent on the agency of ordinary women and men who are also important actors, as I have shown above. Most importantly, however, the focus on cross-border trade enables us to envision other economic possibilities that can mitigate the inequalities produced by corporate global trade.

Without a gender lens, it would be impossible to correct the myopia of the mainstream literature on economic globalization. The gender lens enables us to see how women constitute a majority of cross-border traders; how they use the opportunities of economic restructuring, despite the patriarchal obstacles they encounter in the process; and how, in so doing, they are shaping economic globalization as much as economic globalization is impacting them. Women's economic activities alert us to how local and regional markets are linked with the global capitalist markets. Thus, cross-border trade is an integral part of global trade, not just an anachronistic, "pre-modern" practice existing alongside corporate trade, as some analysts argue.

In fact, by creating a market and selling Western consumer products in urban and rural areas, without the high advertising costs used for the urban markets in the North, these cross-border traders are subsidizing TNCs. Moreover, the demand for products by cross-border traders has led to a burgeoning of manufacturing in many countries. These manufacturers produce knockoffs of popular Western brands. So cross-border traders are supporting noncorporate producers in many economies around the world. This picture of global trade is not only more nuanced than a picture that focuses only on TNCs, but also highlights women as actors shaping globalization.

As I have shown above, women have engaged in this trade out of necessity as well as innovation. In the process, they have developed social networks and new collective identities that have empowered them as individuals and as members of communities.

A similar rethinking of political globalization is the focus of the next chapter.

NOTES

1. The data for this chapter come primarily from secondary sources and the websites of several networks of cross-border traders in Africa. I was also fortunate to have a colleague at the University of Illinois, Professor Mahir Saul, who had done surveys of cross-border traders in five countries of West Africa.

2. Such cross-border trade is usually referred to as "informal cross-border trade." I do not use the term "informal" as it privileges the modern, industrial economy, just as economic globalization privileges the multinational corporate sector. My aim is to undermine such hegemonic thinking so we can imagine other possibilities. Moreover, it is this "informal" economy that provides a livelihood for most people, even in our globalized world. Hence, I use the term informal in quotation marks and only when citing others who use it.

3. Microcredit programs give small loans, from $50 to $100, primarily to women in the developing world, but increasingly also to poor women in the United States, to start their own businesses. Women are targeted because they are a good risk, with over 90 percent loan repayment, and women's loans go toward family welfare, as opposed to those given to men. Microcredit programs emerged in the 1970s in India and Bangladesh and have now become a much-touted strategy by all development and aid agencies, despite the strategy's limitations in actually enabling women to get out of poverty or become socially empowered. (See, e.g., Cotler 2005.)

4. My rethinking of agency owes much to Mahmood's (2004) articulation of Egyptian women's agency in the piety, or mosque, movement. In this movement, she suggests that Egyptian women inhabit religious norms rather than merely resisting or reproducing them.

5. Unless otherwise noted, the following sections are based on these works: Cheater 1998; Cheater and Gaidzanwa 1996; CORN and AFSC 2004a,b,c,d; Darkwah 2007; Morris and Saul 2005; Muzvidziwa 2001; Peberdy 2000, 2002; Peberdy and Crush 1998; Peberdy and Rogerson 2000.

6. The Zambian currency is the kwacha ("K"). $1 = ZMK 3,430. The currency in Zimbabwe is the Zimbabwian Dollar or ZWD $1 = ZWD 101,999.

7. The pula ("P") is the currency of Botswana. $1 = BWP 5.93.

2

Transnational Feminists

Between Global Gender Justice and Global Social Justice[1]

NEW GLOBAL/TRANSNATIONAL POLITICS[2]

> Ours is not the top-down model of the WTO or an international bureaucracy like the UN. Our globalization comes up from communities, from women and men trying to make homes and community in a time of intense change. Instead of working in isolation, as they had to do in they past, they are partnering, collaborating, networking, cooperating, sharing, linking, traveling, writing, publishing, World-Wide-Webbing, and e-mailing.
>
> The Huairou Commission is proud to be an agent in the globalization of grassroots women's organization, one that not only remembers the roots of human society, but nurtures and nourishes them, that encourages far flung solidarity and enables transfer of knowledge, skills and people's resources from one situation of urban poverty to another. (Huairou Commission Newsletter 2000)

As the above quote suggests, there is a new kind of political globalization underway. Analysts of political globalization, or what is also referred to as *global civil society* or *globalization from below* (e.g., Appadurai 2000; Falk 1999), focus on how processes of global economic restructuring have decentered the traditional actors in the international arena, namely the nation-states, and brought to center stage new actors such as NGOs, transnational social movements, transnational advocacy networks, and transnational coalitions (e.g., Keck and Sikkink 1998; Khagram, Riker, and Sikkink 2002; Moghadam 2005; Tarrow 200). Scholars of political globalization, thus, focus on transnational activism as the key political development in global politics.[3]

Transnational activism refers to political activism that transcends national boundaries either in terms of issues addressed, actors involved, strategies and methods used, or the perspective of the activists. Most social-movement scholars link the development of transnational activism to economic globalization (e.g., Keck and Sikkink 1998; Khagram, Riker, and Sikkink 2002; Moghadam 2005; Tarrow 2005). In particular, economic globalization is seen both as a source of common grievances—such as rising inequality due to neoliberal trade policies that benefit the rich countries of Europe, North America, and East Asia (the Global North) at the expense of cheap labor from poorer countries in Africa, Asia, and Latin America (the Global South)—and as a source of opportunities for activism, via international institutions such as the UN, as well as through information and communication technologies such as the Internet, which enable activists to connect rapidly with others across the globe.

But the importance of nonstate actors is not the only new dimension of political globalization. These new actors are forming new kinds of political organizations. The most important are transnational networks (e.g., Moghadam 2000).[4] The assumption of political actors today is that all politics is at once local and global. Hence the local—in terms of issues, identities, strategies, methods, targets of protest, and worldviews—is influenced by and, in turn, shapes the global. This understanding of politics has led to the dominance of transnational networks in global politics. Transnational networks appeared in the international women's movements before the emergence of information and communication technologies and before they became the dominant type of organizational form in transnational politics in general (e.g., Ferree and Tripp 2006; Moghadam 2000; Naples and Desai 2002).

Among the major political strategies used almost universally by all transnational political actors is that of forming alliances or solidarities with other political actors. The transnational advocacy networks tend to come together around exchanging information, research, and policy formulation. The transnational social movements form solidarities around joint mobilizations and tactics (e.g., Khagram, Riker, and Sikkink 2002; Moghadam 2005). Transnational solidarities partly grow out of the logic of transnational politics. You can't have politics across borders without forming alliances. But beyond the organizational logic is also the commitment to social justice that underlines transnational politics. Political actors today see all issues as interconnected and hence recognize the need to work with other NGOs, social movements, and networks to address both local and global issues. This intersectional analysis, and what is called "transversal politics," is also something that the women's movements pioneered (Yuval-Davis 2006). That transnational politics includes new actors, new kinds of organizations, and new strategies is not contested. This is evident in the burgeoning literature on global politics (e.g., Burbach 2001; Naples and Desai 2002; Keck and Sikkink 1998; Khagram, Riker, and Sikkink 2002; Sklair 2002; Ferree and Tripp 2006; Waterman 2002). What most of them miss is the contribution of feminist women's movements[5] or a gendered analysis of this global politics. Paraphrasing Mahatma Gandhi,[6] I would argue that contemporary transnational politics are essentially feminist politics in terms of their logic, organizational structures, and strategies of change. They borrow what contemporary transnational women's activism developed over the Decade for Women, from 1975 to 1985.

Furthermore, the mainstream debate on political globalization sees the new nonstate actors as responding to economic globalization, or "globalization from above." Hence, these analysts consider political globalization as "globalization from below" and nonstate actors as resisting globalization from above (e.g., Falk 2000; Guidry, Kennedy, and Zald 2000; Hamel et al. 2001; Khagram, Riker, and Sikkink 2002). When you look at women's transnational politics, you see women not only resisting globalization but also enacting alternatives; so women's transnational politics is not just reactive to globalization but is constitutive of new globalizations (as the quote at the outset of this chapter shows). In the rest of the chapter, I show how feminists around the world have contributed to transnational politics, moving between global gender justice and global social justice, and in the process have articulated new alternatives in the time of neoliberalism and neo-conservatism.

TRANSNATIONAL FEMINIST ACTIVISM

Transnational feminist activism takes at least three forms: transnational activism around the UN conferences; transnational grassroots activism; and transnational activism around global justice. All are dominated by what I call the *transnational activist class*. First I define this class, and then I focus on their transnational activism.

While there were transnational activists in the nineteenth and early twentieth centuries in the antislavery, women's, socialist, and anticolonial struggles, they did not constitute a class, per se. In the earlier transnational phase, activists were primarily men and women from Europe and the United States, with few from other parts of the world. Hence, the flow of ideas and strategies was primarily from "the West to the rest." Moreover, while they interacted with each other and were influenced by each other's work, they did not consciously articulate a transnational vision, except in the case of the socialist struggle. Nationalism framed a lot of their strategies and ideologies, and most of their work was within that context.

Today's transnational activists are men and women from many parts of the world, though there is a domination of some countries in some world regions, such as South Africa, Kenya, and Ghana in Africa; India and the Philippines in Asia; and Brazil, Peru, and Mexico in Latin America.[7] The flow of ideas and political strategies is multidirectional. Today there are structural mechanisms for ongoing transnational articulations, facilitated by the information and communication technologies—such as Internet and Web-based chat rooms, Listservs, discussion boards, and instant messaging—and an expansive network of funding through private and public foundations, which enables the maintenance and reproduction of this class. Finally, the processes of contemporary globalizations have reached many more parts of the world, leading to both a "global consciousness" (e.g., Giddens 1999) and the necessity for transnational response for local and global changes.

Transnational activists are educated, middle-class men and women, primarily from the Global North but also from select countries in the Global South (Moghadam 2005). These men and women are recognized as providing a critique of, as well as alternatives to, transnational politics dominated by inequalities of power between and within the North and the South. They share many social and demographic characteristics with the "transnational capitalist class" (Sklair 2002). According to Leslie Sklair (2002), the transnational capitalist class is composed of four factions: one made up of corporate executives; another made up of state and interstate bureaucrats and politicians; the third made up of professionals; and a consumerist faction made up of merchants and the media.

The transnational activist class comes primarily from the professional faction but also from the state and media factions. Many of the activists circulate among these three factions, moving from international NGOs to the UN to the academy and/or running for political office. What sets members of the activist class apart from the capitalist class is their explicit political identity and work. Some activists work to reform the system; others, in anarchic tradition, develop alternatives alongside the system; and still others work to develop a counterhegemonic politics. But all of them work within transnational networks and share a global consciousness.

Today we are in the midst of a paradigmatic shift in our understanding of social institutions and social relations (Seidman 2000). Most social analysts argue that contemporary globalizations have not only led to a reorganization of the economy on a global scale but have also shaped a new social imagination in which we are expected to rethink social relations and identities as fluid, flexible, and deterritorialized, rather than as confined to bounded spaces (e.g., Guidry, Kennedy, and Zald 2000; Hamel et al. 2001). While most theorists recognize that globalization is uneven and affects men and women in different parts of the world differently, we are nonetheless all urged to understand how the local and global, both fluid categories, inform each other, and how their interplay shapes both.

For activists, this has meant going beyond the usual nation-state-based movements. But the terrain of transnational activism, given its reliance on information technology and expert knowledge, cross-border travel, and dialogic gatherings, privileges educated middle-class activists or "popular intellectuals" (Baud and Rutten 2005) over other movement activists and participants. Popular intellectuals, as opposed to organic intellectuals, are "knowledge experts" who often are formally educated and are usually not from the constituencies/classes on whose behalf they make claims and frame issues, but rather come from the middle classes (Baud and Rutten 2005). The increase in educated women around the world has shifted the gender and geographical makeup of this class. This transnational activism has also been defined as "globalization from the middle," as it is the middle-class educated people moving around the same circuits (Waterman 2002).

For feminist activists, the UN's World Conferences on Women, with their attendant NGO forums and funding, provided the context for contemporary transnational politics. It is to this politics that I now turn.

Transnational Gender Politics around UN Conferences

Women organizing across national borders, as indicated above, is neither new nor specific to contemporary globalization. It is at least a century old, emerging within the context of the old abolitionist, suffragist, socialist, and anticolonial movements (Sinha, Guy, and Woollacott 1999). The contemporary transnational organizing is primarily a product of the UN's Decade for Women (1975–1985), with its four world conferences and NGO forums[8]—1975 in Mexico City, 1980 in Copenhagen, 1985 in Nairobi, and a follow-up conference in Beijing in 1995—and preparatory national and regional meetings.

The four women's conferences[9] and accompanying NGO forums were contentious events with women from the South, not all of whom identified as feminists, who challenged Northern women's conceptions of women's issues based solely on gender and sexuality and insisted on bringing in issues of development, nationalism, and neocolonialism. These differences among women began to be acknowledged, and "solidarities of difference" (Desai 1999) were forged as they continued to meet over the decade and share experiences of inequalities and struggles for justice. These interactions were taking place both among activists at the NGO forums and among government delegates at the official UN conferences. These solidarities were forged through several strategic breakthroughs.

At each UN conference, women's organizations from the NGO forum formed a caucus through which they sought to interact with and influence the UN conference (Bunch and Reilly 1994). The caucus consisted of daily meetings where all women's organizations were welcomed. Here women shared information about what was going on at the UN conference, and how they could ensure that their voices were part of the deliberations and the final declaration that emerged from each conference. Caucus members then interacted with government delegations at the UN conferences to influence them. Gender-friendly governments, such as those of European countries and some Third World countries, were especially targeted for advocacy. Such caucusing has now become normative at UN conferences.

Another important strategic innovation was that of holding a women's tribunal at the NGO forum. The first such tribunal took place in 1975, around the issue of violence against women. Women from different parts of the world stood up and told their stories of violence, which ranged from wife-battering and rape during war to the structural violence of poverty. Following the testimonials of women, prominent judges from around the world were asked to pass judgments and formulate a call to end violence against women. These judgments and declarations were then used by the women's organizations to influence the UN conference. Such tribunals have also become normative at UN conferences and other global gatherings.

Finally, beginning with the first conference, women activists were forming networks with each other. The earliest examples are the International Women's Tribune Center that emerged in 1975, and Isis, a transnational network of women's organizations, which emerged a year later. These networks differed from the international organizations of the early and mid-twentieth century in terms of their organizational structure and functioning. The earlier international organizations were hierarchical and federated structures. Women's networks, by contrast, were horizontal alliances of autonomous women's organizations. More importantly, the contemporary transnational networks included women from the South as well as the North, and feminist practices evolved in dialogue, often contested dialogues, between women from the North and the South (Moghadam 2000).

It was the 1985 conference in Nairobi that marked a shift from contention to solidarity between women from the North and the South; and by the fourth conference in Beijing in 1995, women, despite their differences, had found a common language in the human-rights framework. "Women's rights are human rights" emerged at the World Conference on Human Rights in Vienna in 1993 but became paradigmatic in Beijing. Thus, the UN conferences and then the UN's specialized agency meetings, such as the "Convention on Elimination of all Forms of Discrimination Against Women" and the "Committee on the Status of Women," became the prime sites of this new phase of transnational activism. Most who attended the NGO forums accompanying the UN conferences were middle-class, educated women from international NGOs; donors; academics; and activists. Most of the transnational feminist networks, such as "Development Alternatives with Women for a New Era" (DAWN), "Women in Development

Europe," and "Women Living Under Muslim Law," emerged during the post-1985 period and consolidated the network model of transnational organizing, which then became the dominant form in transnational politics (Moghadam 2005).

At the Huairou forum in 1995, only women from the major international NGOs and donors were involved in interacting with the official conference in Beijing. But what marked a communicative breakthrough at the Huairou NGO forum was the presence of the Internet. The Association for Progressive Communication, a network of organizations providing Internet services to civil-society organizations, provided free Internet to the 30,000 delegates at the forum. This enabled women's organizations at Huairou to send home daily reports and bulletins and thus reach many more women around the world. Thus, the Huairou NGO forum in 1995 marked the beginning of a communicative strategy that combined old and new media and enabled many more women to participate in transnational politics. Chapter 3 on the new cultures of globalization addresses this in greater detail.

In the 1990s, following the Decade for Women, the UN held a series of world conferences, beginning with the World Summit on the Environment in 1992, the World Conference on Human Rights in 1993, the World Social Development Conference and the World Population Conference in 1994, and the UN Habitat Conference in 1996. In each of these conferences, transnational women's networks that had formed during the Decade for Women were an active presence, and they brought with them networking strategies that they had developed in the UN women's conferences, such as caucuses, tribunals, and Internet communications. At all these conferences, women's networks demonstrated that the environment, social development, population, and habitat were all women's issues, and that without a gender perspective none of these issues could be addressed successfully.

Thus, from 1975 onward, women's voices and networks became a prominent presence at the UN and on the global stage in general. What did women's transnational activism at the UN conferences achieve? One of the most important achievements of the three decades of women's activism around the UN has been the emergence of a "global gender equality regime" (Kardam 2004). The regime consists of norms, conventions, declarations, and legal mechanisms for gender equality, supported by the nearly 200 member nations of the UN. The Convention on Ending All Forms of Discrimination Against Women, signed in 1977 and ratified by over 155 nations—the United States has still to ratify this convention—and the Beijing Platform for Action are two important documents that set out what member nations have committed to in terms of legislation and other structural and institutional changes to ensure gender equality. Many countries have enacted legislation, instituted women's commissions and ministries, and made headway in addressing gender inequality.

Yet the implementation of this regime is uneven, not only around the world but also within the UN itself (www.un.org/womenwatch/daw/csw/index .html). Given the continuing inequality of women in all realms around the world, it is ironic that another significant achievement of women's transnational activism has been the emergence of *gender mainstreaming*, that is, the ensuring of gender parity and a gender lens as the dominant policy framework for governments, UN agencies, and other multilateral organizations such as the World Bank. Gender mainstreaming, however, should more accurately be called "mainstreaming women and women's perspectives." For "gender mainstreaming" has been translated only to mean hiring more women and trying to analyze the impact of policies and programs on women. Gender mainstreaming has not focused on how existing structures and policies are gendered male. So gender mainstreaming ends up being about women. Men's gender, and how it frames politics and policies, still remains invisible.

Partially in recognition of this uneven application of gender mainstreaming and the theoretical shift in the development literature from women in development to gender and development, the UN agencies began to note the importance of involving men and boys in gender equality. One of the earliest signs of this shift was in the Beijing Platform for Action, which emerged from the 1995 Fourth World Conference on Women in Beijing. The Beijing Platform noted that men and boys should actively work for gender equality. Following that, all development policies began to address the role of men and boys in gender equality.

In 2004, the Commission on the Status of Women highlighted this move by focusing its 48th annual meeting on "the role of men and boys in achieving gender equality." Robert Connell (2004), one of the experts who participated in the CSW meetings in 2004 in New York City, offered theoretical as well as practical reasons for this shift. He noted that while gender equality had understandably been primarily a women's concern, it was clear that gender power was relational, and so men, as "gatekeepers" of this power, had to be brought on board. Involving them explicitly would also reduce their resistance to change; and, finally, they too had much to gain from ending gender inequalities, even though giving up the dividends of patriarchal privilege would not come easily. But even bringing in men and boys did not explicitly address the issue of men and boys as gendered beings.

This one-sided gender-mainstreaming perspective has also deeply influenced the major social movements, particularly the global justice movements. Almost all contemporary global justice movements include a commitment to ensuring women's representation and a women's perspective in their programming. But most fail to see their movements, activists, and strategies as gendered male. As Marianne H. Marchand (2003) notes in her analysis of the gender of global resistance, women organize as women but men rarely organize as men, even when they are working for gender equality.

Another important contribution of this phase of feminist transnational organizing is the articulation of transnational feminism as a theoretical and political perspective. For feminists, transnational activism was not just a scalar shift of activism. Rather, it was a new understanding of the myriad axes of power that created inequalities between men and women but also among women themselves based on race, class, religion, region, and sexuality, among other differences. Such an intersectional analysis led to the need for a transversal politics: a politics based on dialogue and cooperation among differently positioned activists, who are able to shift their understanding and make horizontal and vertical alliances across differences (Yuval-Davis 2006). Such a normative transnational feminism predates Seattle and the global justice movement by a decade and is key to the development of transnational activism.

Thus, the major gains of women's transnational activism at the UN have been discursive, both at the policy and movement levels. In terms of global politics, however, the major contribution of women's transnational politics at the UN has been in defining and consolidating transnational activism as a participatory political process. Strategies developed at the various UN conferences, such as women's caucuses, tribunals and testimonials, and workshops, have become common practice among transnational networks. Finally, developing new communication strategies based on "old media" such as daily newsletters, radio, and video documentation and combining them with new media, namely, the Internet, has also become normative in global politics.

Women's transnational activism at the UN conferences, however, has been fraught with contradictions. Chief among them is that despite the commitment of the world's governments to the global gender equality regime, and improvement in some areas like education and political participation, the state of the world's women had not improved much by 2005, ten years after the Beijing conference.[10] They are still among the poorest, least educated, least healthy, and least powerful groups in all countries.

Another tension is the reproduction of inequalities and influence among women from the North and the South. These stem from several factors. The location of UN offices in New York and Geneva, Switzerland, has meant that women's NGOs in the United States and Western Europe have easier access to and familiarity with the UN. Even the various conferences that have been held around the world have been dominated by women's NGOs from the United States and Europe (e.g., Desai 2002; McLaughlin 2004; Mendoza 2002).

A cautionary note that Biljana Kasic (2004) sounds, writing from the former Yugoslavia, is that in the process of transnational feminism, feminists in the former Soviet bloc, like feminists from the Third World before them, are adopting feminist strategies and feminist issues that are dominant in the

West, such as violence against women. This makes them visible, but also incorporates them as "victims" and the exotic other of the West. Moreover, only certain kinds of feminists get incorporated into the "expertise exchange industry," in which the terms of debate are set by the West and in which visibility is gained at the expense of commercial exploitation. Violence against women, rape, and trafficking become the entry points for Western feminists and for visibility of Eastern women's experiences and issues.

The activism around the UN has also privileged educated women's voices from both the North and the South. Most of them are committed to women's equality, but have few connections with poor women's groups. Hence, the global gender equality regime has provided many educated women with good employment opportunities in NGOs, UN agencies, and government bureaucracies; opportunities for travel and interaction with other feminist activists; and opportunities for framing transnational feminist activism. While transnational activists speak for their constituents, most are removed from them except as service providers or gender experts. Clearly, institutions and transnational feminist networks like Development Alternatives with Women for a New Era (DAWN), the Women's Environment and Development Organization (WEDO), and others have played an important role in advancing the feminist research and policy agenda at the UN and other international spaces (Moghadam 2005). But transnational feminism at the UN has not led to redistributive policies or transformation of societal structures and institutions. These goals bring together grassroots women's organizations as they shape both global policy formulation and local transformations, as I show below.

Women's Transnational Grassroots Activism

Forging strategic partnerships to advance the capacity of grassroots women worldwide to strengthen and create sustainable communities.[11]

This is how the Huairou Commission defines its work. It is a network of networks that brings together grassroots women's networks from different parts of the world. Its main aim is to develop partnerships of grassroots women's organizations and networks with local governments, academics, NGOs, UN agencies, and donors, that is, to bring together the powerless and the powerful, so all partners can share their particular powers and expertise to transform society.

The Huairou Commission was formed in 1995 following the Fourth World Conference on Women in Beijing and its accompanying NGO forum in Huairou. It was a response to the lack of a grassroots women's presence and grassroots women's voices in the UN conferences, which were dominated by middle-class and professional women and activists. While all the conferences dealt with issues of poor women, they were framed and presented by professional women. This, the Huairou Commission felt, silenced the style and expertise of grassroots women and prevented them from developing their own power base, from the local to the transnational levels.

Discussions about the lack of grassroots women had begun a decade earlier at the Third World Conference on Women in Nairobi in 1985, among women from Cameroon, Kenya, India, the Philippines, and the United States who worked with grassroots women and felt frustrated with the lack of those voices. This discussion led to the formation of Grassroots Organizations Operating Together in Sisterhood (GROOTS) in 1989, and the Huairou Commission in 1995. The Huairou Commission's core networks include the Asian Women and Shelter Network, GROOTS, the Habitat International Coalition–Women and Shelter Network, the International Council of Women, WEDO, the Women and Cities Network, and the Women and Peace Network.

The Huairou Commission uses a three-pronged approach in its work: development of partnerships through local, regional, and global exchanges among grassroots women; collaborative projects between grassroots women's networks and institutions at local and global levels; and network communication that enables grassroots women's organizations to share and find partners for their work. The Huairou Commission brings grassroots women's voices into global politics by building two kinds of capacities: those of grassroots women's organizations and those of their communities. The former is defined as "building people's information base; decision making capacities; negotiation and articulation skills; technical know-how; managerial skills; and capacity to reflect and evaluate development processes." The latter is defined as: "improving a political and legal environment which enables grassroots participation in development processes; developing gender sensitive community institutions." Of their various programs, I focus on two: the "Global Women's Learning Academy" that focuses on the capacity building of women's organizations, and the "local-local dialogue," whose aim is the capacity building of communities.

The Global Women's Learning Academy is an annual meeting where grassroots women from around the world gather to share and learn about local solutions and local innovations with which they may want to experiment in their own communities. The academies began in 2000 and have been held each year on a different theme. Grassroots groups are selected based on their interest and expertise on the theme of the year. They lead the academy and make presentations to the larger group in formal and informal settings. Then the assembled women work in small groups to identify common challenges and craft policy recommendations. While some professional women attend and sometimes make presentations, all the sessions are organized and facilitated by grassroots women themselves. Policy makers are invited to join the academies at the end, to listen to their recommendations and to find ways to incorporate the recommendations in their work. Thus, the main aim of the academy is "to harvest knowledge from the women, spread their solutions, converse with policy makers, and develop new strategies."

The first academy was a survey of what grassroots women had been accomplishing at the local level. Forty-two groups from around the world met over a six-week period and presented their local work, leading to the Huairou Commission's first publication, *Our Best Practices*. Since then academies have been held on land, the work of women in responding to HIV/AIDS in sub-Saharan Africa, and the Istanbul+5 Habitat conference.

The 2006 academy was held in Vancouver, Canada, just before the World Urban Forum, from June 12 to 16. The themes of the 2006 academy were participation in local decision making; cities that work for women and their families; women building resilient communities after natural disasters, conflicts, and health crises like HIV/AIDS; and strategies and partnerships that center women. One hundred and fifty community leaders from thirty-three countries, as well as indigenous community leaders from Canada, met for five days to teach and learn from each other about their efforts, successful and failed, and to make policy recommendations both to the World Urban Forum that followed and to policy makers in their own communities. They also crafted recommendations to address the UN's Millennium Development Goals.[12] Their recommendations were as follows:

> If you pay attention to us and include us as equals, we will achieve the Millennium Development Goals, and much more. Based on our experiences, we suggest the following actionable ideas:
>
> 1. Consult grassroots and indigenous women as key experts.
>   Given our longstanding contributions and demonstrated knowledge and skills in improving the quality of life and building democracy, grassroots women must be represented as experts in all global, regional and national dialogues.
> 2. Establish new funds for grassroots women's Peer Exchanges, public spaces and organizing.
> 3. Donor Dialogues: International aid agencies should schedule dialogues with grassroots women leaders and local authorities to redirect funds & programs.
>   Grassroots women's groups have been filling the gaps and working with their local authorities to access and redirect resources for effective local problem solving.
> 4. Support grassroots and local authority collaborations and Local-to-Local Dialogues to sustain women's participation in local decision-making.

Local to local dialogues are locally designed strategies whereby grassroots women's groups initiate and engage in on going dialogues with their local authorities for negotiating issues and priorities; Joint planning; Developing on going partnerships.

(http://www.huairou.org/assets/download/Events/WUFIII/Final_2006_ Academy_Report.pdf downloaded August 4, 2008)

The Grassroots Women's International Academies are based on peer learning—on sharing and reflection—the principle of which is that women possess knowledge that needs to be recognized as such and spread to others through methodologies that work for them. The academies also enable women's grassroots organizations to produce knowledge and methodologies that can be used by professionals and academics. Thus, this knowledge production can become a source of income for the grassroots women, as they produce manuals and curricula that are available for sale.

Another aim of the academies is to shatter common myths about grassroots women in the political arena, including the myth that "grassroots" means small scale. As some of the presentations at the academies have shown, many projects in India and Asia have involved thousands of villages and thousands of women and men. Another common myth is that grassroots solutions are low skilled and low tech. Here again, the academies have shown that women have learned high-skilled jobs such as masonry, construction, and engaging in research and evaluations. Finally, it is assumed that grassroots women are learners and not teachers. But, as the academies have shown, if we change our definitions of *teaching*, grassroots women are just as capable of teaching about their daily lives as are professionals and experts.

So the purpose of these academies is to make grassroots women visible and influential. The peer exchanges provide space for "creation and reproduction of knowledge that is owned and nurtured and replenished by the women themselves" (Menon 2001, 1). They allow the larger world to see the "magic of women's realities" (Menon 2001). But more importantly, they enable women to influence local and global policies, as well as giving them access to what Menon (2001) calls the "culture of influence," namely, government officials, bureaucrats, academics, think tanks, and the UN.

The second major initiative of the Huairou Commission that builds capacities of communities takes the form of the local-local dialogues and partnerships. This initiative was the result of the collective efforts of many women's organizations. Among the initiators of the idea were Sheela Patel, director of the Society for the Promotion of Area Resource Centres (SPARC), and Prema Gopalan, director of Swayam Shikshan Prayog (SSP; Self-Learning Experiment). Both SPARC and SSP are grassroots women's organizations that work

with poor women in the slums of Bombay. According to Achola P. Okeyo, a
Huairou Commission partner,

> dialogues become the means to open up channels of policy discussion for
> grassroots communities while at the same time amplifying an understanding
> of why gender matters, why participation is key to local decision-making and
> how democracy can be achieved in a very practical way on a common forum
> where anyone can have an idea about what needs to be done to solve common
> problems in a conflict free way. (Okeyo quoted in Capacity Development of
> Grassroots Networks to Become Effective Partners in Local Governance for
> Poverty Eradication: Lessons from Below. (http://www.huairou.org/assets/
> download/Capacity_Building.pdf downloaded August 4, 2008)

Local-local dialogues start with enabling grassroots women to engage and
negotiate with local authorities and institutions. The hope is that such dialogues will be supported and institutionalized and will also contribute to
collaborative action research projects that can facilitate real transformations
in the lives of women and men in communities around the world. I cite
some examples of such dialogues involving Bombay-based women's organizations and other women's organizations in Asia.

India: Toilets in Indian Cities

There simply are not enough toilets in Indian slums. Women literally have
nowhere to go, or are forced to walk long distances for privacy. Conditions are
unhygienic and safety is a serious concern. The National Slum Dwellers Federation (NSDF) and Mahila Milan (Women's Association), supported by an
NGO called SPARC (Society for the Promotion of Area Resource Centres), have
been working in Mumbai and other cities in India for over a decade to address
the problem of sanitation for the urban poor.

When toilets in slums become unusable it happens for many reasons. The Federation has found that sanitation solutions designed and planned by the government are unviable. Communities need to participate in developing sanitation facilities because they know what will and won't work in their communities. By
experimenting with different options and building their skills in construction and
negotiation, communities have developed a model in which communities plan,
construct and maintain their own toilets in their settlements.

The State brings sewers and water supply to the site and pays for the materials. In the city of Pune, a partnership between the municipal government, NGOs and community-based organizations has built more than 400
community toilet blocks. They have also demonstrated the potential of
municipal-community partnerships to improve conditions for low-income
groups.

Some women community leaders took on contracts themselves and managed the whole construction process, supported by engineers and architects
from SPARC. It took a while for the women in each community to develop the

confidence that they could manage this process. As one leader, Savita Son-awane, noted, "In the beginning we did not know what a drawing or a plinth was. We did not understand what a foundation was or how to do the plaster-ing. But as we went along, we learnt more and more and now we can build toi-lets with our eyes closed." Over time, these women's groups gained confidence and as they learned how to deal with the local government bureaucracy, they became active in dealing with other government officials. They also kept a close watch on costs.

This program enabled the reconfiguring of relationships among the city gov-ernment, NGOs and communities. The city government recognized the capac-ity of community organizations to develop their own solutions, supported by local NGOs. The city authorities changed their role from being a toilet provider to setting standards, funding the capital cost of construction and providing wa-ter and electricity.

Women and the Changing City in Penang, Malaysia

The Local-to-Local Dialogue in Malaysia was undertaken jointly by Penang Heritage Trust with support from the Asia West Pacific Network for Urban Con-servation (AWPNUC). George Town, Penang, is a historic port city of great cul-tural diversity. In the last 30 years, the Control of Rent Act protected inner city communities inhabiting about 10,000 pre-1940 buildings from market forces, while new housing areas expanded in the periphery. With the Repeal of the Control of Rent Act at the turn of the millennium, many households are fac-ing rental hikes and evictions, accelerating the decline of population in the in-ner city neighborhoods. In addition the plan to restore the community market also threatens the situation of residents in the area.

The Penang Heritage Trust (PHT) undertook the Local-to-Local Dialogues in George Town, Penang, to explore how women were affected by the changes in the city and how local government can improve quality of life and opportuni-ties for women. The first phase of the Dialogues consisted of small dialogues hosted by non-governmental organizations and community groups to identify and prioritize issues. This was followed by the main Local-Local Dialogue, which brought together various stakeholders from community and govern-ment. Broad policy recommendations as well as concretized proposals were put forward to pursue follow-up actions. Approximately 200 participants par-ticipated in the Local-Local Dialogue, of whom nearly three-fourths were women.

The event provided a forum for the community women—normally mem-bers of the silent majority—to learn more about the city's plans to restore the Cambell Street Market, and to voice their opposition to top-down planning which ignored their needs. Community women were supported by women professionals who asserted that removing the market would violate principles of planning, as it would undermine the economic and social base of the com-munity. The politicians and bureaucrats both were compelled to recognize that the maintenance of the community market was necessary to support the gov-ernment's vision of a "living heritage city."

The Dialogue also highlighted the fact that it was not only buildings but also people, that had to be "sensitized" to the special needs of the disabled community—and this included the police, bus drivers, civil servants etc. Traffic crossings, for example, have to be accessible not only to the disabled, but the elderly and the very young too. However, this is perhaps the first time that the case for disabled access policies and implementation was being presented before a public forum. Both government and ordinary people were educated about the attitudinal and technical requirements of providing an enabling environment, and the State Women's Development Committee and local authority promised to follow up on the dialogue.

Allegations of unfair allocations, inefficiency and corruption in processing social housing applications have been circulating for some time. However, previous community surveys and mobilization helped participants communicate their concerns clearly. The affected applicants who were present at the event stood by their complaints. They highlighted the plight of the urban poor, representing hundreds of other poor families and women-headed households who were suffering the same predicament. Politicians and bureaucrats promised to monitor the situation more closely.

Overall, there was a realization of the inter-relatedness of urban issues. Accessible design, heritage conservation, public safety, more social housing and improved security of tenure, better community amenities, would all be improved with more community feedback, bottom up planning and public participation in decision-making.

Securing the Right to Live in the City, Kathmandu, Nepal

The Local-to-Local Dialogue in Nepal was undertaken by LUMANTI–Support Group for Shelter in Kathmandu, which focused on the issues surrounding women and the security of shelter.

The Local-to-Local Dialogues process initiated by LUMANTI in Kathmandu was divided into two phases: the preparation of Family Identity Cards and a two-day workshop. The family ID cards of the squatter families were prepared and jointly issued by the Women's Federation (Nepal Mahila Ekta Samaj) and Squatters' Federation (Nepal Basobas Basti Sanrakshan Samaj). The provision of these identity cards to squatters was a historical breakthrough as it symbolized the city's recognition of the rights of squatters as citizens, thus providing them with a form of secure tenure. On the second day of the workshop the Mayor of KMC distributed the ID cards to the squatters in Balaju community.

These initiatives from Asia have in common ongoing dialogue as the basis for their success. Their experiences point to the fact that wherever communities have influenced government authorities to respond to their needs by involving communities in planning, designing, implementing and monitoring programs, it has been because of an ongoing engagement through which women's groups and their communities have been able to devise solutions that work for both sets of actors. In other words, partnerships with authorities require an investment in a local dialogue process. (Huairou Commission 2002, 10–12).

Based on dialogues similar to the ones presented, the Huairou Commission has developed a tool kit for facilitating such local-to-local dialogues and actions among women's grassroots organizations. The tool kit, from which the above examples were cited, includes examples of such dialogues around the world and outlines the main principles and strategies of such dialogues. For a meaningful dialogue, three main principles are highlighted: seeing poor women and men as citizens, not clients or beneficiaries of government; seeing local government as allies in their work; and focusing on transformation and redistribution of power (Huairou Commission 2002, 13). Based on these principles, the tool kit outlines strategies that women have used successfully. These strategies include collective action, capacity building, building alliances, and demonstrating capacities.

Thus, linkages or partnerships are the core of the Huairou Commission's methodology. *Partnership* has become a much maligned term in the development literature since 2000, when UN agencies and donors have used the term to refer to corporate partnerships in which the poor are seen primarily as economic agents in a market-driven development (e.g., McMichael 2005). But the grassroots women's organizations and the Huairou Commission have redefined the term several times in response to their experiences of forming such partnerships.

In their initial strategic plan in 1998, they defined "New Ways of Partnering" that were based on recognizing the inequalities among partners and focusing on building capacities to address those inequalities. In the initial code of conduct for partners, the grassroots women's side was heavy on demand rather than exchange, as they saw themselves as having little power (Leavitt 2000). But when the local-to-local dialogues were initiated in 2002, grassroots women saw themselves as having power as well, power based on their daily struggles and innovations. This shift was reflected in the 2004 Global Women's International Academy, in which women saw that their knowledge benefited both themselves and their communities, and thus they were equal partners despite their lack of traditionally valued power. In the most recent strategic plan, 2003–2006, the Huairou Commission has focused on creating new learning programs and education programs that can provide financial resources for the grassroots groups.

Not only have women redefined partnerships, they have also initiated them at various levels, from the local to the global. The kinds of partnerships developed by grassroots women include rebuilding community partnerships, such as rebuilding after war, earthquakes, and slum evictions; developing physical infrastructures such as intergenerational centers and public spaces; engaging in economic development by acquiring market-place space for women vendors and developing women's construction businesses; developing AIDS-related knowledge and care; engaging in political partnerships to develop gender budgets and antiviolence ordinances; and forming global partnerships for slum-dwellers' rights, safe cities, and empowerment as development. In these various partnerships, women's organizations have also outlined the responsibilities of various partners, as indicated in table 2.1.

The work of grassroots women's organizations has also impacted other transnational movements around the world. In Bombay, two things were important with regard to the emergence of the youth movement, Youth for Unity and Voluntary Action (YUVA; the acronym also means "youth" in several Indian languages):

1. Gender issues were central to the organization and its self-definition, and the focus was on developing women's and girls' leadership.

> We believe that development is a continuous struggle to create a humane society, which sustains all human beings, as well as nature; where women,

Table 2.1.

Investments by Local Authorities	Commitments from Grassroots Women
Gender budgets	
• Allocate a percentage of your budgets for women's participation and projects.	• We will prepare budget proposals for grassroots women and negotiate agreements.
• Evaluate use of gender-budget funds.	• We will report on the impact of allocations on the community.
• Institutionalize women's participation in the construction of budget.	• We will increase our ability to participate in constructing budgets.
Land and Housing	
• Legislate women's property rights.	• We will vote for those who support our property rights.
• Involve women in planning, design, and construction of low-cost housing communities.	• We will bring our local knowledge to planning and commit to building our capacities.
• Support women's community self-help systems.	• We will continue to invent self-help systems.
• Ensure urban environments that are safe for women, as defined by women.	• We will define what makes cities safe for us.
• Create a network of partners to expand good low-cost housing solutions.	• We will work with all partners to expand good low-cost housing solutions.
• Provide basic services to low-cost housing communities.	• We will monitor the provision of basic services.

(From Huairou Report to Partners on GWIA, 2006, www.huairou.org/assets/download/Events/WUFIII/Final_2006_Academy_Report.pdf.)

men and children enjoy universal human rights. (from YUVA's Mission statement www.yuvaindia.org/programs/ accessed on April 6, 2006)
2. The process of working with the poor was important to the organization.

> YUVA will empower the oppressed and the marginalized by facilitating their organizations and institutions towards building equal partnerships in the development process, ensuring the fulfillment of the human right to live in security, dignity and peace. (from YUVA's Mission statement www.yuvaindia .org/programs/ accessed on April 6, 2006)

While women's leadership is emphasized to ensure equality, YUVA's gender work includes men in defining and practicing gender equality. "Men too are victims of patriarchy and should be engaged in redefining their masculinity as well as addressing gender inequality in their work."[13]

Thus, gender issues are being incorporated by other grassroots movements as well and have influenced the global justice movement, as I show below.

Transnational Women's Activism and the Global Justice Movement

To most analysts, the global justice movement is represented by the protests against the WTO that began in Seattle in 1999, and which have continued at the annual meetings of the WTO, as well as at World Bank meetings and G8 summits.[14] Initially, the mainstream media labeled these protests "antiglobalization," as they opposed the corporate, market-driven economic globalization that was leading to increasing disparities within countries and between countries. However, as activists and analysts indicated, the activists, too, are a product of political and economic globalizations, and they are not opposed to the interconnectedness of people or to the flow of ideas and images. Rather, they are opposed to the unrestricted flow of capital, production, and services and the restricted flow of labor and people. In short, they are opposed to corporate globalization and are in fact in favor of a globalization that is for people rather than for profits.

The global justice movement has consolidated since Seattle and is made up of many movements and networks across the world. While scholars debate whether a global justice movement exists, most activists feel a sense of solidarity with the varied ways in which social movements, NGOs, and other groups are working around issues of global justice (Eschle 2001).

It was in the name of the global justice movement, and as an alternative to the World Economic Forum in Davos (where leaders of corporate globalization met), that the first World Social Forum (WSF) was called in January 2001 in Brazil. It met in Brazil from 2001 to 2003, moved to India in 2004, and returned to Brazil in 2005. It was organized as several polycentric forums around the world in 2006, and in 2007 it met in Kenya (http://www.forumsocialmundial.org.br/main accessed august 4, 2008). There are links on the main page to its charter and who we are that addresses these issues.[15] Today, the various regional and even national WSFs are more important than the global gathering.

The first WSF in 2001 in Porto Alegre, Brazil, was organized by the local Workers Party. It was a response to two contradictory tendencies in Latin America in the 1990s: increasing democratization and the spread of neoliberal globalization. The latter generated structural crises and inequalities, while the former provided a space to address these growing crises. The protests against corporate globalization that began in Seattle in 1999 and continued through the end of the decade created new networks and led to the consolidation of the global justice movement.

The WSF was organized as a democratic space in which movements, NGOs, and people from around the world could share their struggles and reflect on alternatives. The language of the WSF stresses process, and autonomy from state and parties (even though it was an initiative of a leftist party in Brazil). Feminists were active in the WSF from its inception, and gender equality was stressed as one of the important aspects of global justice. Yet the first two forums did not have as many sessions on gender, nor were women in prominent positions in the international organizing committee (de Sousa Santos 2006). It was to address this lack of attention to feminist issues that women's groups from Latin America, Asia, and Africa met informally at the 2003 forum to discuss the idea of "Feminist Dialogues."

Thus, the Feminist Dialogues were a response on the part of feminists attending the WSF to its lack of attention to feminist issues and the lack of women in all arenas from the International Council and national organizing committees to the roster of plenary speakers. Although elimination of gender oppression and the insights of feminist practices and processes were highlighted in the WSF charter (http://www.forumsocialmundial.org.br/main/charter of principles accessed August 4, 2008), the first three WSFs held in Porto Alegre, Brazil, from 2001 to 2003 did not reflect this commitment in the makeup of the International Council or the national organizing committee, the two bodies that plan the WSF; in the gender breakdown of the keynote speakers; or in the sessions on gender—despite the large presence of women as participants in most of the movements represented at the forums. It was to challenge this marginality that feminists from seven feminist networks in Africa, Asia, Latin America, Europe, and the United States[16] met "under a tree" during the WSF in 2003 in Porto Alegre to organize a plan of action that would engender the forum and make it feminist in its focus, method, and participants (Desai 2005).[17]

The first Feminist Dialogue was held a couple of days before the 2004 WSF in Bombay (http://feministdialogues.isiswomen.org/index.php?option=com_content&task=view&id=27&Itemid=38 accessed August 4,

2008). Since then it has been held twice, in 2005 in Porto Alegre and in Nairobi in 2007, two days prior to the forums. The rationale for holding the meeting before the forum is as follows:

> In having the meeting before the WSF we hope to achieve a two-way political exchange: firstly, we hope to effectively intervene in the broader WSF process as feminists organizing for change, and to establish strategic and politically relevant links with other social movements. As a site of resistance,[18] the WSF is one of the most dynamic spaces available to us as feminist activists and it is important to participate in it while at the same time retaining our autonomy within the FD. We also are hopeful that the idea of the FD can be used to encourage various regional level meetings or to participate in the different forums we are engaged in as part of our ongoing work of linking up with other movements. Through the FD we do not seek to come up with unified positions or perspectives. While a certain minimum consensus is necessary to maintain the cohesion of the meeting, we think that the value of meetings such as the FD lie in bringing forth debates and differences that provoke us to reflect, reassess and recast our analyses and strategies, collectively as well as individually. The FD can be a platform that strengthens our diversities as well as our common politics. (http://feministdialogues.isiswomen.org/index.php?option=com_content&task=view&id=26&Itemid=37 accessed August 4, 2008)

Thus, the feminists who initially met to address the issue of marginality of women's and feminist issues pursued a two-pronged strategy: to ensure feminist presence in the International Council and the national organizing committee of the WSF, in order to make sure that feminists and feminist concerns would be central to the WSF; and to create an alternative space, the Feminist Dialogues, alongside the WSF, in order to provide feminists with an opportunity to engage in dialogue.

The first strategy had a dual approach. One aspect of the strategy took the form of behind-the-scenes negotiations between the feminists and the Brazilian and Latin American organizations—mostly labor and peasant organizations, as well as the political party that had organized the first forum and hence was disproportionately represented in the International Council and the Brazilian organizing committee. This strategy clearly bore fruit, as the Indian organizing committee and International Council that planned the 2004 WSF in Mumbai each had a fairly high percentage of feminists, and the WSF in Mumbai was one of the most "gender equal" WSFs to date. More than half the sessions focused on gender, about half the plenary speakers were women, and about half the Indian organizing committee was composed of women activists. But the success of the Mumbai WSF did not continue in the 2005 WSF in Brazil and the 2007 WSF in Nairobi. My sense is that as feminists focused their energies on organizing the Feminist Dialogues, the strategy of gendering the WSF took a backseat.

The second aspect of gendering the WSF consisted of organizing feminist sessions at the forum. One of the sessions that the Feminist Dialogues had organized in India, and which continued in Brazil, was an intermovement dialogue among the feminist, gay, lesbian, transgender, labor, and *dalit*[19] antiracism movements. The intermovement dialogue at the WSF was an example of taking intersectional politics seriously. Its aim was to enable each movement to reconceptualize its vision in relation to those of other movements. A representative from each movement had a chance to reflect on the ways in which they had succeeded and failed in addressing the issues of the other three movements. Given the setting, all the representatives spoke of building alliances; but none of them engaged the questions posed by the Feminist Dialogues regarding the relationship of their movement to the other three movements. There was no effort to think through ongoing coalition building for redistributive efforts at local or regional levels. The participants and most of the panelists were women. Here were feminists who had become autonomous from parties and other movements and were now seeking to build solidarities based on a position of strength and a well-developed feminist perspective.

But if this session was an indicator of coalition politics, it did not seem very promising. Solidarities with other movements have become the hegemonic movement strategy. But as the intermovement sessions at the forums in 2004 and 2005 showed, movements haven't done the serious work: namely, the work of rearticulating their visions to integrate other visions; reorganizing their movements to include others; and rethinking strategies to address issues of all inequalities, such as inequalities of class, race, gender, and sexuality, among others.

At the 2007 Nairobi WSF, the Feminist Dialogues discontinued this intermovement session and organized a rally and other feminist sessions. The rally was well attended but, again, mostly by those who had already attended the Feminist Dialogues. There were many other sessions on gender and feminist and women's movements at the WSF that were independent of the Feminist Dialogues. So the Feminist Dialogues' attempts to ensure feminist presence at the WSF are restricted to working with feminist networks that are part of the Feminist Dialogues, and do not involve reaching out to other women's groups and movements. Most of the Feminist Dialogues' energies are focused on the Feminist Dialogues per se.[20]

The Feminist Dialogues take place over three days, which are organized around several opening and closing plenaries and "buzz groups," or small-group discussions around specific themes or questions. One of the opening plenaries at all the Feminist Dialogues is about their history and process, which helps orient new participants. Other opening plenaries are thematic.

The thematic plenary in Porto Alegre was entitled "Further Provocation: Moving Forward with Our Multidimensional Identities and Internal Diversities" (Feminist Dialogues 2005). Most of the presenters and the inter-locutors were academic feminists, who laid out a critique of where we were in the present neoliberal conjuncture. The thematic plenary at the Feminist Dialogues in Nairobi in January 2007 was called "Transforming Democracies" (Feminist Dialogues 2007). This plenary addressed the contradictions and limits of formal liberal democracy and the possibilities of liberal democracy through participatory methods such as gender budgets, as well as participatory methods at public, personal, and interpersonal levels within our families, organizations, and movements.

In addition to the plenaries, the Feminist Dialogues consist of buzz groups and small-group discussions around themes emanating from the plenaries (Desai forthcoming). The purpose of these small discussion groups is to provide an opportunity for participation and dialogue to a larger number of women attending the gathering. While there are difficulties of language and translation, both literal and metaphorical, the groups do provide a forum for discussion, though not always for strategizing for political action.

While the Feminist Dialogues involve only a small number of feminists and activists at the WSF, they make an important contribution in terms of engaging the global justice movement and ensuring that feminist issues and practices are key to that agenda. The global justice movement today is more mature, has elaborated a politics of alliance, and has linked the issues of peace and globalization.[21] The U.S. war on Iraq helped mobilize this coalition. The WSF is an important site; and while it emerged as a space of dialogue and sharing, it is now a global network that has survived the post-9/11 surveillance. And looking at the discussions at the various regional forums in 2006, it appears that the WSF is moving in a more political direction. The presence of women's movements, especially the political ecology and indigenous women's movements, is an important part of this shift toward a more political direction.

RETHINKING POLITICAL GLOBALIZATION

Most of the mainstream literature on political globalization focuses on how economic globalization has reshaped "politics as usual" in two important ways:

1. It has brought nonstate actors such as NGOs and transnational social movements onto the global political stage.
2. It has also changed the geography of local politics. Political actors now operate at local, regional, and transnational levels.

Focusing on the women's movements, we see that they were at the fore-front of defining political globalization in terms of the transnational per-spective, the new organizational structures, and the new strategies of polit-ical globalization. The Decade for Women, 1975–1985, brought together women's organizations from around the world, and the feminist principles that they had developed across their respective local contexts facilitated the formation of a new transnational perspective for political action, new orga-nizational structures, and also new strategies. Primary among them was the commitment to an intersectional analysis and transversal politics. The con-tentious experiences of dealing with differences among women in women's movements in the North and South enabled the transnational women's gatherings to form solidarities across differences.

In addition to having this transnational political perspective, transna-tional feminists were the first to develop transnational networks to share ex-periences and to strategize for political action at multiple levels, based on nonhierarchical, informal structures and participatory processes. Transna-tional feminist networks were formed before the information and commu-nication technologies made such networks de rigueur in the various transnational movements.

Finally, transnational feminists developed strategies—such as tribunals, caucuses, grassroots women's networks, and partnerships with other move-ments and local authorities—that articulate autonomous spaces (like the Feminist Dialogues in conjunction with the WSF) as both a critique and an alternative, and which have now become common in global politics. Hence, global politics have to be recognized as feminist politics. Most liter-ature on political globalization recognizes the importance of women as po-litical actors but does not necessarily acknowledge that transnational women's activism has shaped the nature of global politics, from its transna-tional perspective to its organizational structures and strategies.

Even feminist analysts often underestimate the impact of transnational women's activism. Feminist scholars have recognized for decades that the issue of power is understood both in terms of the structural power of the state and the capitalist economy and in terms of the discursive power of micropolitics (Piper and Uhlin 2004). Yet recent feminist analyses of women's transnational activism have all lamented its focus on and success in shaping discursive power (e.g., Desai 2005; Pearson 2004; Rai 2004). Ruth Pearson (2004) and Shirin Rai (2004) note that transnational feminists have actively engaged the institu-tions of global governance and made important contributions to policy changes, from gender mainstreaming to gender budgets, gender codes of ethics to microcredit to the "Maria Tax";[22] yet there is growing gender inequality. Pearson (2004) argues that in part this is a result of conflating academic fem-inist analysis with feminist politics, and that while analysis is needed to un-dergird political action, it is not political action by itself.

But they fail to recognize that feminist discourses and feminist practices have shaped global political practices. Furthermore, this critique stems in part from focusing on women's transnational activism at the UN. Most analysts do not take into consideration transnational grassroots women's activism. As I have shown above, grassroots women have also learned to capitalize on the openings provided by globalizations, to organize and build their capacities by partnering with local authorities, professionals, and others with influence and resources, and to develop alternatives to address inequalities. Grassroots women's organizations have recognized that under neoliberalism the state has become the market, and so women's emancipation depends on negotiating with the state and the market in more complex ways (Simon-Kumar 2004).

In a similar vein, Gita Sen (2005) argues that during the heyday of transnational organizing around gender justice, when gains were made in terms of policies and commitments at the international level, neoliberalism, which was pro–gender justice, was the dominant global discourse. Now with the ascendancy of neoconservatism, gender justice is under attack. The relationship between gender justice and social/economic justice has been a contentious one in feminist theorizing as well as activism. While intersectional and transversal politics are articulated as a means of bridging them, in practice they are seldom visible. Either gender issues are silenced or they exist in isolation. But I would argue, based on the complex terrain of transnational women's activism, that women have defined a neoradical politics that refuses to separate issues of gender justice and global justice, by bringing issues of each side to the other.

NOTES

1. Data for this chapter came from participant observation at several UN conferences, World Social Forums, and Feminist Dialogues; interviews with many transnational feminists over the past decade; the websites of many transnational feminist organizations; and secondary sources.

2. While the term *global politics* could encompass politics such as that of terrorists as well as religious fundamentalists, my focus here is only on global social justice politics.

3. I prefer the term *transnational*, meaning "across many nations," rather than *global*, as most NGOs and social movements are not truly global in their scope, even if their commitment is to global justice. As in many things "global," NGOs and social movements also reproduce existing global inequalities. Hence, most "global" NGOs are still based in the United States, Western Europe, and select countries in Africa, Asia, and Latin America.

4. Moghadam coined the phrase "transnational feminist networks" and was among the early voices that recognized this new form of political organization.

5. While feminism is still a contested term, I use it to refer to those women's movements that challenge gender inequalities in all domains and are committed to gender justice.

6. Gandhi described his nonviolent struggle for India's independence as a "women's war," as it was based on "women's" values of nonviolence and sacrifice (http://www.mkgandhi.org/articles/articleindex.htm accessed August 4, 2008).

7. With the exception of the Latin American countries, all these countries are English speaking, and that could partly explain their dominance. The political cultures in these countries also explain their prominence.

8. The first NGO forum alongside a UN intergovernmental conference took place in 1972 at the Earth Summit. Following that, the women's conferences consolidated the presence of NGO forums at each of the conferences. NGO forums were organized simultaneously with the UN conferences, to provide NGOs and social movements an opportunity to meet and discuss the issues being addressed at the UN conferences.

9. The UN conferences are for government delegations, though increasingly many governments include activists and NGO members as part of their official delegations.

10. The Commission on the Status of Women organized a "Beijing Plus Ten" review at its 48th session in March 2005 and found that in most areas of women's life, much remained to be done; and that in some areas there had been backtracking, due to religious fundamentalisms, the U.S. war on Iraq, and increased militarism in general following the war on terror (http://www.un.org/womenwatch/daw/csw/ 48sess.htm accessed August 4, 2008).

11. Unless otherwise cited, all quotes in this section are from the Huairou Commission website, www.huairou.org. and its "our knowledge" link which was accessed during April 2006.

12. The Millennium Development Goals (MDG) are eight goals that the world's governments formulated at the General Assembly session of the UN in September 2000. Among the goals are elimination of world poverty by 2015, education and health care for all, women's equality in all societies, universal access to information and communication technologies, and citizenship rights for all (http://www.un .org/millenniumgoals/ accessed August 4, 2008).

13. Interview with Minar Pimple, founder of YUVA, April 17, 2006.

14. The Group of Eight (G8) are the eight richest countries in the world; they meet every year to chart global economic directions. They are Canada, France, Germany, Italy, Japan, Russia, the United Kingdom, and the United States.

15. I have firsthand knowledge as a participant in three of the WSFs: Bombay 2004, Porto Alegre 2005, and Nairobi 2007.

16. The seven networks were Development Alternatives with Women for a New Era (DAWN), the Women's International Coalition for Economic Justice (WICEJ), Articulación Feminista Marcosur (AFM), the National Network of Women's Autonomous Groups (NNWAG), the African Women's Development and Communication Network (FEMNET), INFORM–Sri Lanka, and Isis International–Manila.

17. My analysis of the Feminist Dialogues is based on my participation in two of three FDs held to date; on informal conversations with participants and members of the coordinating group responsible for organizing the FD; and on the papers cir-

culated by the FD, and the FD website. In 2005 I was invited as a facilitator of the FD in Porto Alegre. In 2007 I applied to participate in the FD in Nairobi.

18. It is curious to me that feminists and others consider the WSF as a "site of resistance." It is a gathering of social movements where most engage with other movements already in the network; where the event is structured around fairly academic sessions presented by mostly middle-class, educated activists; where most of the so-called grassroots people engage in a forum of their own outside the sessions based on cultural performances and selling crafts and other products; and where there are rallies to mark the opening and closing of the forum, reminiscent of such rallies at the Olympics. In the WSF charter (http://www.forumsocialmundial.org.br/main .php?id_menu=4&cd_language=2 accessed August 4, 2008)://www.forumsocia), only one of the fourteen principles addresses opposition to neoliberal globalization, capitalism, and other forms of oppression, and a search for alternatives. All the other principles are about pedagogy, process, democratic participation, and network and other solidarities.

19. *Dalit*, meaning "oppressed," is the term chosen by the ex-untouchable castes of India to refer to themselves.

20. Several North American and European funding agencies, such as the Global Fund for Women and Mama Cash, support the Feminist Dialogues. The funds support rental of conference space; food and meals; travel for some participants; and travel, room, and per diem for members of the coordinating group, facilitators, and plenary speakers.

21. Interview with Walden Bello, April 13, 2006.

22. Pearson (2004) proposed that this tax be levied by national governments on exporters, in proportion to the number of women in the export zones. The tax would be used specifically for gender equity for women workers in the export zones, and also for women in the economy as a whole.

3

Modemmujers and the New Cultures of Globalization[1]

GLOBALIZATION AND CULTURE

Eclecticism is the degree zero of contemporary general culture: one listens to reggae, watches a western, eats McDonald's food for lunch and local cuisine for dinner, wears Paris perfume in Tokyo and "retro" clothes in Hong Kong. (Lyotard quoted in Harvey 1989, 87)

Most discussions on culture and globalization assume very narrow definitions of both. *Culture* is defined by food, music, clothing, and values, or a very narrow mix of what Raymond Williams (1963) called the *aesthetic* elements of culture (i.e., music, art, and literature) and the *anthropologic* elements of culture (i.e., meaning making and daily practices). I focus on the anthropologic definition of culture, as meaning making that sustains daily living.

Similarly, most definitions of *globalization* see it is as a contemporary and modern phenomenon. Some may date it to 1492 and the voyages to the "New World" (e.g., Wallerstein 2004), while others date it to colonization (e.g., Chase-Dunn 1998), or to the 1970s (e.g., Sklair 2002). I, along with Jan Nederveen Pieterse (2004) and others, see globalization as a deep-historical process[2] that includes the ancient migrations of populations across the world, cross-cultural trade, the spread of world religions, and the spread of technologies through cultural contact between various regions of the world. The long-term historical perspective challenges two common assumptions in the globalization debate today: first, that globalization is a product of Western modernity; and second, that globalization is an extrinsic force rather than a historical process intrinsic to all cultures in varying forms and to varying extents.

These two common assumptions mean that the debate on culture and globalization has been dominated by three views (Nederveen Pieterse 2004): *cultural differentialism*, or lasting difference; *cultural convergence*, or growing sameness; and *cultural hybridization*, or ongoing mixing.

Cultural differentialism was popularized by Samuel Huntington's "Clash of Civilizations" (1993). Huntington views cultures as emerging from "civilizations" (e.g., Judeo-Christian, Islamic, Chinese) with distinct values. When these civilizations come in contact with each other, they clash because of their fundamental differences. Not only does this view ignore historical reality, in which these cultures were not isolated from each other but rather influenced each other, it also uses dogmatic assumptions about culture to view contemporary geopolitical issues and crises, particularly between the United States and the Middle Eastern countries.

The cultural convergence perspective was formulated around the same time by George Ritzer (1993), who described what he called a "McDonaldization" of society. He argues that the principles of efficiency and sameness that are the hallmarks of fast-food restaurant success are now shaping other realms of society and culture, and are being exported to the rest of the world. Americanization replaces Westernization as the process of cultural diffusion.

The third perspective, hybridization, regards cultural mixing as not only a historical process but also part of the human condition. "The essence of the human condition is a fundamental connectedness with parts of the universe across space and time" (Clark 1997 quoted in Nederveen Pieterse 2004, 25). In this view, cultures have been mixing and producing new hybrid structures, identities, and organizational forms since *Homo sapiens* first spread from Africa to populate the world (see Appadurai 1996). Hybridity is also variously known as *mélange, creolization, syncretization,* or *glocalization* (e.g., Cox 1997; Robertson 1992; Featherstone 1990).

There is a growing critical literature on hybridity that indicates its unevenness, or the unequal power relations intrinsic to it. In response, Nederveeen Pieterse (2004) has theorized hybridity as a continuum, where one end is *assimilationist hybridity*, based on mimicry and adopting the dominant culture, and the other is the *destabilizing hybridity* that challenges the mainstream (like the hybridity theorized by Gloria Anzaldua, 1990).

While the perspective on cultural hybridity is sensitive to the way gender plays a part in its construction, its focus tends to be more on consumption, particularly of food, music, and dance, such as Japanese salsa, bhangra rap, or klezmer flamenco.

But in these formulations, hybridity is an outcome, a product (Nederveen Pieterse 2004). I define hybridity as a process of collective, intercultural communication. There is very little understanding of hybridity in daily meaning making, or the more anthropological sense of culture. As more and more political battles are fought via the medium of culture today, it is important that we focus on this form of hybridity, in addition to the hybridity of music, dance, food, and clothing. I argue that the spread of information and communication technologies[3] is enabling women and men to create new cultures of globalization, or new hybrids between cultures and technologies. Thus, the new cultures of globalization are at once "virtual" and "real" and facilitate local, place-based, and transnational, virtual cultural citizenship.

These new cultures of globalization are invented and imagined based on traditions as well as modernities; combine new organizational structures with new forms of communication; circulate transnationally; and illuminate alternative cultural possibilities that blur the distinctions between the aesthetic and everyday senses of culture. What information and communication technologies make visible is what all cultures with a strong oral tradition know, that "the process of exchanging bits of information and creating new constructs out of the old bits goes on all the time—whatever the technology" (Namjoshi 1999, 373). As Suniti Namjoshi (1999) notes:

(1) Technology does not equal civilization, (2) Passage through time does not equal progress, and (3) Literacy does not equal education. To put it more dramatically: India has a highly civilized, highly illiterate population. (372)

By making it possible for illiterate people to engage in cultural creation, information and communication technologies further the feminist possibilities of globalization. These new cultures of globalization are created to address the inequalities of class, gender, race, and sexuality, that is, as a means of expressing cultural citizenship.

To illuminate these new cultures of globalization, I turn to the analysis of cultural citizenship and then "cyberfeminism," feminist activism on the Internet, as one expression of cultural citizenship; and finally show how it informs the new cultures of globalization, using the examples of Independent Media Centers and the Women's Networking Support Programme.

CULTURAL CITIZENSHIP IN THE CYBERAGE

The concept of *cultural citizenship* has evolved from the efforts of the state and cultural institutions to bring "culture" to the urban masses in the West; to its use by dominant groups in the Global South to shield people from "westoxification" and to gain recognition for their "traditional culture"; to its appropriation by marginal groups to acquire cultural rights (Chaney

2002). The concept, however, reflects a narrow, nineteenth-century view of culture as bound to nation, as homogenous, and as an uncontested category. But as anthropologists have shown us over the past forty years, there is no single culture, even in a nation-state. Culture is a contested terrain as well as an invented one, and it is often a response to marginalization as well as to opportunities provided by globalizations.

So in this context of multiple and fragmented cultures, I define cultural citizenship, not only in terms of politics of difference, recognition, and respect, but as a group's ability to shape common cultural discourses. Borrowing from Williams, Nick Stevenson (2003) defines *common*, not as "same," but as the ability of common people to influence cultural dialogues and institutions.

Cultural citizenship, then, is a contested desire for communication in an information society, which builds new institutions and opportunities for dialogue. Stevenson (2003) calls this an *ethical cosmopolitanism* (as opposed to the cosmopolitanism arising from class privilege, mobility, and hedonism that reinforces class boundaries), which is about living with difference, an art of life rather than of travel and consumption. Therefore, even locally rooted folks can be cosmopolitan in their ethics and be part of imagined communities and virtual communities that are facilitated by the technologies of communication, particularly the Internet.

What I call the "new culture of globalization" has resonance in what Wendy Harcourt (1999) calls the "new culture in cyberspace," where women from across the world meet in cyberspace in new global networks but are still rooted in their local cultures and politics. Arturo Escobar (1999) emphasizes the need to understand the new cyber networks and cultures in relation to what he calls "place based political practice." Technology is important; but it is only a tool, and change depends on power relations in the real world. Hence, he argues, the relationship between cyber culture and political change has to be politically constructed. He calls this political construction the "feminist political ecology of cyberspace." Central to this construct is the ability of the Internet to connect people, rather than to separate them by creating real and imagined boundaries. To the extent that these networks "foster different ways of interacting and relating, of thinking about life, gender, justice, and diversity" (50), they will be critical to the political project of rethinking gender and globalization. It is to these feminist, Internet projects that I now turn.

FEMINISM AND CYBERACTIVISM

By the mid-1990s, the Internet was widely available, and feminists from around the world had already forged solidarities, as I have shown in chapter 2. Hence, there was a corpus of feminist theories and practices that was brought to bear on this new technology, and cyberfeminism was invented. The term *cyberfeminism* was first used by Sadie Plant (1997) and is defined as activism to change the power differences between men and women in the digital discourse (e.g., Hawthorne and Klein 1999). Others, like Harcourt (1999) and Donna Haraway (1997), define cyberfeminism more broadly as the use of technology for addressing gender inequalities in digital discourse, as well as in the material and ideological spaces. Bela Bonita Chatterjee (2002) articulates cyberfeminism as the relationship of the Internet, gender, and sexuality with identity and its relationship to feminism as a political project. All these varied definitions of cyberfeminism highlight connectivity, critique, and creativity as important components of a critical, cyberfeminist politics. As with most issues, however, feminists are divided about cyberfeminist politics. The key feminist arguments for and against the Internet can be divided into three categories: *technological*, *theoretical*, and *strategic*.

The technological arguments highlight the nature of the technology itself as a key to women's liberation. This position is best exemplified by the work of Plant (1997), Sherry Turkle (1995) and Dale Spender (1995). For Plant, cyberspace is essentially female; and, although it was designed by men, it will ultimately undermine male power. This transformation, she argues, does not need feminist intervention or identities. Virtual reality will do it all by its design, a technologically determined position.

Plant (1997) claims that cyberspace is about weaving virtual selves and realities. Turkle (1995) and Spender (1995) similarly argue that cyberspace is woman-friendly, as it is based on communication, consensus, and community: all practices at which women excel. All these theorists believe in "cyberutopia" and are seduced by its possibilities in imagining an alternative, women-centered, postgender world (Chatterjee 2002). These scholars' analysis is supported by cyberfeminist activism such as "women with attitude," or "bad grrls" who use the Internet for utopian purposes as artists, designers, academics, and software designers for gender equity. (See womenwithattitude .tripod.com and www.badgrrls.com.) The emphasis is on virtual identities and individual use in daily lives, not on a collective movement.

But this cyberutopia that many cyberfeminists avow is based on the privilege of wealth, education, and time that most men and women, in the South as well as the North, don't have. So while affluent Western feminists might see themselves as cyborgs as they create and design professional and personal identities on the Net, women who assemble those computers experience cyborg identities as long hours of hard work assembling products most will never use (Luckman 1999). As Sara Kember (2003) notes, cyberfeminism, to be meaningful, needs an ethics, a politics, and a history, rather than "cyber drool."

As opposed to the individualistic "cyber drool" of the previous argument, another technological argument focuses on the collective knowledge that is possible given the technology's abilities. *Connectivity*, or many-many interactions and communications, produces new ways of "commonspace thinking" (Surman 2004), which foregrounds the power of the collective. Sharing power, Surman argues, leads to synergy, creativity and the gift economy on the Internet. Commonspace thinking, however, is confined to the virtual community. Without connection to real communities, one cannot have real social change. Technological arguments tend to foster a politics based on virtual and discursive identity politics coming mostly from white, Northern feminists. It tends to focus on the ability of the Internet to foster myriad new identities that allow freedom for women in cyberspace—that is, its *expressive* use. It is in response to the limitations of virtual, or purely cyberbased, activism that feminists and other activists have articulated strategic arguments.

The strategic argument for cyberfeminism differs from the technological one in its focus on how the Internet can be used for women's empowerment, and in its explicit connection between virtual activism on the Net and place-based activism on the ground. The strategic argument for cyberspace has developed in three different literatures: feminist literature, women and development literature, and technology and minority literature in the United States. I review the arguments in each of these three literatures.

Within feminism, this argument has been made most widely by Susan Hawthorne and Renate Klein (1999) and Gillian Youngs (2005, 2006), among others. Their main argument is that while information and communication technologies are a product of transnational capitalism, women and others can use them to challenge that regime. That is, "the master's tools can dismantle (or at least remake) the master's house." As I will show below, this is possible because the technology was developed not only by the masters but also by "geeks."

Youngs (1998) argues that the Internet provides a way for women to develop collective knowledges and practices for social transformation, by providing a safe communicative space in which they can transcend public/private, geographical, and national boundaries. No doubt many feminists will challenge the notion of the Internet as a safe space, given its use for cyber-stalking, pornography, and trafficking, among other threats. Yet the Internet has helped women in developing international connectivity, discursive authority, and cyberidentities (Youngs 2005, 2006), as is the experience of women in international development.

The women in international development and Internet discourse, primarily conducted by UN agencies like the World Health Organization, the UN Educational, Scientific, and Cultural Organization, the Food and Agricul ture Organization, and the UN Development Programme (Asiedu 2006), sees women's access to the Internet primarily as a means to eradicate poverty and promote development and, secondarily, as a medium to address issues of human rights. E-development now joins e-commerce and e-governance as the future of our information society (Colle 2004 cited in Asiedu 2006). The focus of this discourse is on the best practices for providing women access to the Internet through *telecenters*, or collective computer facilities. The Internet becomes a means to the end of development, as opposed to its potential to organize cyberpower to determine the kind of development, culture, and politics that people want.

Within this literature, gender integration is seen as important for ensuring women's access to information, training, and business opportunities (Jorge 2000). Hence, specific best practices—such as 50-percent ownership by women, outreach, financial and physical accessibility, relevance, confidence building and training, and participation—are culled and promoted. In the case of Africa, women are being turned into consumers by the various information and communication technology programs funded by donors, the UN agencies, and governments (Robins 2002).

But it is not enough that women have access to the Internet. For if the project of development itself is neocolonial, then what does having access to development mean? Who has the ability to define that (Gajjala and Mamidipudi 1999)? Thus there needs to be a process of dialogue, where women enter as equals and where they are encouraged to be creative and to dream their own utopias. It is in response to such goal-oriented articulations of development that cyberfeminists construct another discourse in which women are engaged in cyberspace not only to alleviate poverty—important as that is—but also as a means of gaining social, cultural, and political power that enables them to define the kind of development they would like for their communities, instead of being forced to follow the neoliberal model of globalization that the West imposes on all countries around the world. So where, when, why, and how women enter cyberspace is crucial to the future of cyberfeminism, for cyberspace can be used productively by people concerned with social change and who do not have the luxuries of wealth, education, and time (Escobar 1999; Harcourt 1999).

The final literature that contributes to the strategic arguments for the use of the Internet for cyberfeminism comes from minority communities in the United States. It draws upon community, race, and class scholarship. The main focus of scholars and policy makers in this literature has been on "the digital divide," or the differential access that privileged white communities have to the Internet, as compared with communities of color. But as cyberfeminists argue, the problem is not the digital divide per se, but how the digital divide is addressed, and for what purpose.

The community-based cyberfeminists are also utopian, but their utopias are collective and are about addressing inequalities. Cyberfeminists working in African American and Latina communities in the United States foreground class and race among women and make these central to using the Internet for social change—as opposed to those cyberfeminist discourses that emanate from white, middle-class, and educated women in the North, primarily the English-speaking North, which are about virtual selves and virtual identities (e.g., Everett 2004; Harcourt 1999; Kvasny 2003; and Wright 2006).

Based on work with black women in the United States, the strategic argument made by scholars is that for poor women, the Internet is a means of "ascension" or liberation, as it provides opportunities for community-based educational and economic projects. Anna Everett (2004) calls this hybrid cyberfeminism "cyberwomanism," where women use the Net for activism. Cyberwomanism, according to Everett, is "making do," a tactic of sharing cyberpower with those who don't have it. For poor, urban, black communities in the United States, cyberpower, the ability to communicate via the Internet, is necessary for democratic politics today (Alkalimat and Williams 2001). An important way for poor, disenfranchised communities to access it is through social capital and community centers that support people with information rooted in the social organization of the community. All forms of capital should be brought to bear on developing social capital that will enable the development of cyberpower.

But in poor communities, access to the Internet has to be provided in conjunction with skills that poor people need for economic and social empowerment (Gordo 2003). This was demonstrated by the project "Plugged In."[4] Based on community demands, Plugged In began programs for children, teens, and adults. The programs engaged the groups in producing knowledge that was turned into products for sale, and also created a community dialogue.

Based on a study of a community telecenter in a poor, black community in Ohio, Lynette Kvasny (2006) found that it is not the digital divide that is the problem as much as digital inequality. She found that if the center does not provide access to other, nondigital services such as education, health care, and employment, access to the Internet is not very meaningful. It just reproduces privilege and the social order. Conditions under which skills are acquired are as important as the context in which they can be invested.

Hence, some feminists are not convinced about the strategic use of the Internet. Marisa Belausteguigoitia Rius (1998) argues that women's voices are still excluded: for example, even in the Zapatista movement, you seldom hear the voices of indigenous women. So the old questions of representation, mediation, and ventriloquism still persist. Hence, she argues that the master's cybertools have to be dismantled and deconstructed by feminist cyborgs "to analyze and understand highly sophisticated forms of erasing women's voices." Only then can we achieve the dream of women's command of and freedom in cyberspace to use multiple languages and desires (Belausteguigoitia Rius 1998, 30).

In a similar vein, Susan Luckman (1999) argues that "cyberspace cannot escape the social construction of gender because it was constructed by gendered individuals, and because gendered individuals access it, in ways that reinforce the subjugation of women" (36).

The theoretical arguments about information and communication technologies try to temper the skepticism about the strategic use of the Internet. They highlight the kinship between feminist theory and the possibilities of the Internet. N. Katherine Hayles (1995) and Haraway (1997) argue that for women's emancipation, we need knowledge that is based on interactivity, positionality, and connectivity, and the Internet enables such knowing (Deuze 2003).[5] Escobar (1999) argues that women, environmentalists, and Third World social movements might be more in tune with interactivity, positionality, and connectivity for historical and cultural reasons. This might enable them to make the link between "cyberspace and place, between activity and interactivity, presence and tele-presence, existence and tele-existence" (Escobar 1999, 52).

In a slightly different vein, Youngs (2005, 2006) argues that information and communication technologies will allow for the mainstreaming of feminist theories because they have a lot to offer our current socio-technical lives. In particular, she argues that feminism can contribute to the discourse on the ethics of access. Feminists have shown that the liberal notion of equality is partial, and so we need women and other marginal groups to engage in a discussion of equality. Second, feminist theories have shown how the gendered nature of the history of technology and science silenced women and minorities, as well as rendering them invisible in these spaces. Finally, feminist theory has shown the importance of horizontal networks in enabling and empowering women who did not have power to articulate, and become active agents in their own lives, as well as in the lives of their societies. Thus, as the Internet becomes central to contemporary lives, feminist theories become relevant to all.

The technological, strategic, and theoretical dimensions of cyberfeminism are all visible in the work of the Independent (Indy) Media Centers and the Women's Networking Support Programme. These two examples of new cultures of globalization embody collective connectivity that is interactive and relational, and based on commitment to social justice and cultural citizenship. Both these examples are made possible by the new communication technologies, as well as by social networks, political networks, and projects of activists.

INDEPENDENT MEDIA CENTERS

Indy Media,[6] as their website (www.indymedia.org) notes, is

an international news organization;
a participatory media production and distribution platform;
a decentralized social and digital network;
a people's CNN;
an activist communications network;
an experiment in global democracy;
a social phenomenon;
an advocacy network;
a bulletin board;
an organizing tool;
a chat room;
a laboratory for social and technological innovation;
an incredible experiment in self-governance; and
a pioneer in the communication landscape. (www.indymedia.org/en/static/
    about.shtml accessed April 12, 2006)

And, I would add, Indy Media is a new culture of globalization. Born in
the throes of the protests against the WTO meeting in Seattle in 1999, the
Indy Media movement was made possible by the information and communication technologies (computers, the Internet, and open-source software), as well as the need to create media that represented "communication
from the people" (Vatikiotis 2004). It is both a medium for people to create news as well as an organizing tool for movement activists. The Internet
is not just an efficient means of communication; it is "an invitation to a
new imaginary" (Poster 1999 quoted in Atton 2004).

Indy Media is part of a long tradition of alternative or radical media in
the United States and elsewhere (Atton 2004; Hyde 2002). Its most immediate inspiration, however, was the use of the Internet by the Zapatistas in
1994, both to communicate to the world and to start a dialogue about the
means of achieving radical democracy. Led by Dan Markle and other activists from a host of alternative news agencies, such as Free Speech TV and
Protest.Net, activists used a local building, computers, and the Internet to
provide an alternative reporting of the protests against the WTO in Seattle.

Reflecting the new global culture that it was to become, the software that enabled them to broadcast came from an Australian activist, Mathew Arinson in
Sydney (Couldry 2003). It helped that the WTO meeting was in Seattle, the
home of technology-savvy activists who made it possible to stream live reports
across the world on the Web. The first Independent Media Center (IMC) in
Seattle, through its website, acted as a clearinghouse—of news, photos, and
videos recorded by the protestors—for other journalists and activists.

The IMC in Seattle "laid the infrastructure for a multimedia people's news room" (Hyde 2002). By 2000, following the meeting in Seattle, there were 30 IMCs, in cities primarily in the United States and Canada, and now there are over 142 IMCs, in 53 countries, on every continent, though still heavily in the Global North (Garcelon 2006). The spread of IMCs thus reflects global inequalities of location, class, education, and gender, among others. But it is an important phenomenon, with 100,000 hits daily on the global site and about 2 million hits on the network, and 5 million hits during global events (Mamadouh 2004).

My analysis will focus on the IMC phenomenon in general and IMCs in Latin America in particular. Outside North America and Europe, Latin America has the most extensive network of IMCs, a total of 17 at this writing, with most countries having at least one and some having several. Within Latin America, Brazil has the highest Internet growth (Fuentes and Straubhaar 2001).

What makes IMCs different from other alternative media is that they enable *P2P*, or peer-to-peer exchanges, and *M2M*, many-to-many exchanges—as opposed to most communication, which is from few to many. Thus, ordinary people, albeit mostly educated men and women, become newsmakers and blur the distinction between the production and consumption of news. IMCs erase boundaries between producers and consumers of knowledge, and through horizontal communication develop the emancipatory potential of media. In other words, what IMCs and other new media enable is the "realignment" of the relationship between news media, sources, and audiences (Hyde 2002); or, as Sheri Herndon, one of the founders of the Seattle IMC, puts it:

> The art of communication can be magic. I have seen it happen. I think this is one of our huge challenges, whether it is the World Social Forum, whether it is inside a tiny group of people, whether it is on an e-mail list—to let go of your own stuff, of your ego, to see how you can contribute to the greater good. That is a beautiful thing, because a lot of people haven't ever felt listened to. (Interview with Sheri Herndon quoted in Garcelon 2006, 72)

In addition to peer-to-peer exchanges, Internet and open-source technology enable networking, with myriad possibilities. In so doing, as I show below, they represent a new culture of globalization and cultural citizenship.

What enables Indy Media to do this is open-source software. Graham Meikle (2002) argues that the open-source software that IMCs use reflects the philosophy built into the technology of the Internet. He argues that there is a reason that the Internet is decentralized. It was produced by "geeks who wanted to chat with other geeks (105). Hence, it was developed outside official control and is direct and democratic. This message of democratic participation is built into the form of the medium. Technology is not neutral, but carries with it the intent and the philosophy of its founder. Studies on the history of gender and technology demonstrate this time and time again (e.g., Denis and Ollivier 2003).

The software is open coded so that it can be modified and rewritten by users to meet their needs. The technology also allows innovative ways of archiving and interacting. Though accessibility is limited to those with computers and Internet connections, it enables those with access to interact with over 142 IMCs throughout the world through e-mails and chat channels. The use of open-source publishing, or "copyleft," which does not have individual copyright but uses ideas collectively, is changing the way people have access to information. It allows anyone with access to the Internet to post a news item that is uploaded instantaneously. People become the media. Viewers can not only post articles, but link with editorial, technical, translation, and print teams around the world.

All this relies heavily on volunteer labor and is operated at low cost, as most IMC websites are on servers that are provided either for free or at low cost from cooperative service providers (Coyer 2005a). There is neither an office nor a staff to support, though many local IMCs have a local space and activists who, in addition to maintaining the site, meet regularly. Such volunteer activism allows IMCs to function fairly democratically. There are technical teams and editorial teams that do make decisions; and some news items are hidden, that is, they are not available on the news service but are available in the archives.

Meikle (2002) calls this "unfinished media" that people can use creatively. Herndon (2003) notes that Ferdinand Marcos, the former dictator of the Philippines, used to say that what the government fears is an "expert in communication," and Indy Media is creating thousands of such experts, who are linked to each other across many borders. Herndon sees IMCs as a facilitating space; as an innovative organizational strategy; as a solidarity of diverse networks that are "chaordic" (i.e., constituted by both order and chaos) and that are conscious of being part of a larger network and accountable; as including a variety of ways for people to participate, pool local and expert knowledge, and provide rapid response to fast and flexible events; and as a forum for dialogue, for growing strategically, and for building a movement with multiple and vibrant channels of communication.

At the same time, one should be careful not to read too much into the possibilities of the Internet (Meikle 2002). Radio was a point-to-point communication medium when it started, but it quickly became appropriated by corporate power for broadcasting. And we see corporate interests trying to control the Internet in the United States. How advocates and activists use information and communication technologies and include marginalized peoples will determine their usefulness as a tool for radical democracy (Friedman 2005). Indy Media activists in Australia recommend that we (1) use the Internet tactically but think strategically about its use; (2) be clear about what we want; (3) do not put too much hope in it; (4) be multimedia in our orientation, as most of the world is not connected; and (5) have faith in people and their imaginations (Meikle 2002).

Power to the People

As the IMC website claims,

> The Independent Media Center is a network of collectively run media outlets for the creation of radical, accurate, and passionate tellings of the truth. We work out of a love and inspiration for people who continue to work for a better world, despite corporate media's distortions and unwillingness to cover the efforts to free humanity. (www.indymedia.org/en/static/about.shtml accessed August 4, 2008)

Indy Media's focus is on collective connectivity and participation in creating news that is radical and relevant to people. Indy Media incorporates an organizational strategy, that of a network, as well as an emancipatory ideology that embodies interactive and positional knowledge production across boundaries. Networks have become the dominant organizational structure both inside and outside movement and NGO circles (Desai 2005). The transnational movements, particularly the feminist movements, have been at the forefront of using this structure successfully for advocacy, research, and policy formulation, as discussed in chapter 2 (see also Moghadam 2005).

In forming networks, activists are responding to the need to work at multiple levels, which can be accomplished only through collaborations with others. Thus, the individual IMCs, which often are face-face organizations, are linked electronically to form a network. They do not have a centralized structure, although the Seattle IMC, as the original site and the one that hosts the global website, does play an important role in technical support and linking with the other IMCs.[7] But beyond that, it does not seem to have a centralizing role. This horizontal structure is not just a result of technological possibilities but reflects a commitment to participatory democracy that most new social movements share. Thus, the 17 Latin American IMCs are linked to each other as well as to the 142 around the world.

The IMCs' focus on collectivity is unique, as most globalization and technology literature focuses on the new ways in which individuals can become isolated and alienated from social interactions in the process of being part of virtual communities. Most users of computers in the United States are seduced by entertainment and consumption possibilities provided by the new information capitalism (Dean 2002). This was the case with some cyberfeminists discussed above (Kember 2003).

The IMCs' collective enterprise of solidarity calls into question the focus of both scholars and popular media on individual cultural expressions of globalization. Many media studies scholars lament the fact that such virtual communities lead to more and more individual engagement with the media but not with other people. But what is remarkable about all Web-based sites is that the communities they create are more important than the information they convey (Schrage cited in Hyde 2002). The Indy Media movement is different in that all local IMCs are face-face or place-based communities, in addition to being virtual communities, and they reflect local political culture and concerns.

Another aim of IMCs is to articulate radical, accurate, and passionate tellings of truth. It is an interesting juxtaposition of modern and postmodern understandings of truth as both an objective reality—as reflected in the choice of the word *accuracy*—and a subjective reality—as evident in passionate telling of multiple truths—are highlighted. Indy Media sites do not make claims of objectivity and neutrality. Rather, their websites note that all reporters have their own biases, and so readers should read the stories with a critical eye. These passionate tellings are not just an act of reporting; rather, they are about making the world a better place. In so doing, the tellers are not afraid of working out of love and inspiration, values that are associated with feminine qualities, emotions that are often gendered female. Emotions and passions are central to the new cultures of globalization. For Indy Media, people are the agents of their own lives and histories.

Indy Media is not just a news service; it is a producer of culture as well as a cultural product. People are the communicators who can take charge of media and become producers and makers of news in a literal sense, rather than as targets of news media that have another orientation to truth. This enabling of people to become communicators also mobilizes both definitions of culture, as people give meaning to what is important to them and, in the process, learn a new aesthetic and vocabulary.

Alternative media are often understood in binary ways—as oppositional to the mainstream or as an alternative to the mainstream media—when in fact they are life transforming for the women and men involved in them (Rodriguez 2001). Engaging in producing culture enables people to become creators of their own images, voices, and selves, and transforms them into message producers and storytellers, so that they are not just audiences for other media. Hence, such experiments should rightly be called "citizens' media," to emphasize the cultural transformation. If *citizenship* is defined as active daily engagement in shifting power relations, then we see how citizens' sense of self and access to power shifts in the process of creating news. It may not always lead to social transformation, but it makes people active and engaged, and that has value in itself.

In the almost ten years since its inception, Indy Media has radicalized the way activists communicate. The convergence of activism, the maturity of the Internet, and the domination of corporate globalization galvanized the Indy Media movement (Coyer 2005b). It allows people across vast geographic distances, but with similar political interests, to connect in cyberspace. While Indy Media tries to be as inclusive as possible, there are limits to its strategies.

Limits to People's Power

The main problems faced by the Indy Media movement are limitations with regard to geographic representation, linguistic diversity, and gender balance (e.g., Coyer 2005b; Mamadouh 2004). It is dominated by Northern countries, especially the United States, which has 53 sites; Europe has 40 sites; Australia 11; and Latin America 17. The presence of Indy Media depends not only on access to the Internet and users of the Internet but also on political opportunity structures and political cultures. For example, China, which has a large online population, has no Indy site because of political control; while India, which has an open political culture, has only one site because of infrastructural problems (Mamadouh 2004). Indy Media has tried systematically to address geographical imbalance by transfer of skills and hardware to the South through "caravans,"[8] particularly in South America and Africa. The transfer is not unilateral, as Southern countries transfer content and collective-action skills. But nonetheless, the Indy Media movement reflects, although it tries to address, existing global inequalities.

Linguistic diversity, or lack thereof, is also a problem, in light of the dominance of English. Sixty-eight percent of all websites around the world are in English, with Japanese coming in a distant second at 5 percent. Forty-three percent of the online population uses English, with Chinese a distant second at 11 percent (Mamadouh 2004). The other languages in which Indy Media has interfaces are all European languages with few world speakers; whereas the most commonly spoken languages, such as Chinese, Bengali, and Hindi, have no representation at all. Indy Media is working to provide translation on many sites. Still, the local sites tend to be monolingual, with the exception of the Bolivian and Peruvian sites, which have indigenous Aymara and Quechua languages. The Bolivian site, however, is very incomplete and not always up to date. So while Indy Media is creating a communications commons, for now it is for those who can communicate in European languages.

While there are women in local IMCs, scholars and Indy Media activists complain that it is primarily a male-dominated phenomenon (e.g., Coyer 2005a). It is hard to know what percentage of Indy Media respondents and

consumers are women. There is very little research available on that. It is
male dominated because the technology and the initial setup were male
dominated. Yet all Indy Media sites are explicitly concerned with gender issues, as I show with the Latin American cases.

The response of the Seattle site to 9/11 revealed another limitation of the
movement. Following the attack, the Seattle site carried few "active witness-
ing" reports and many articles by U.S. or U.S.-based intellectuals like Noam
Chomsky, Howard Zinn, and Edward Said. Influenced by the Chomskyan
view of U.S. foreign policy, the site reported mainstream sources and few of
its own reports. The Seattle IMC provided more analysis and interpretations
than activism or reports. That was not true of sites in Latin America and
other places that did reports of their own on the responses to 9/11, as well
as on local protests against the subsequent wars in Afghanistan and Iraq.
What one site carries is not the face of Indy Media as a whole. The aim of
the movement, like feminist movements, is to move away from a hegemonic position for any one particular site.

Another potential limitation of the Indy Media movement is in the area
of participation. Who participates in the Indy Media movement? Is it a
"locked circuit" (Downing 2003)? That is, do activists colonize Indy Media
and close it off to nonactivist audiences? Finally, the Internet, like other radical practices, is open to both commercial exploitation and government
control, as the recent news of Google's and Yahoo's collaboration with the
Chinese government documents.[9] So the Indy Media movement is not a
panacea, but a medium that has potential for democratic practices and social justice.

The Indy Media movement is multiscalar. Activists and audiences can
connect at local-global, local-local, local-regional, or local-national levels,
among other such possibilities, thus enabling the practice of democracy at
many levels. But the movement also faces challenges, such as hackers; government surveillance; and new software—such as open editing, which will
enable anyone to alter another's words. I turn to specific IMCs in Latin
America to show how they are addressing some of these limitations.

Latin American IMCs

Indy Media Brazil was the first site in Latin America, developed in 2000
by seven students at the University of São Paulo. It got started after one of
the students came back from protesting at the Republican Convention in
Philadelphia, where he had encountered the Indy Media movement. The
students had to advertise their presence using fliers, as most people did not
know about them. Thus, they had to first take the IMC to the street before
it could be a Web presence. The São Paulo center later moved from the university to a "squat" building,[10] where participants began to work with poor

youth and single mothers who lived there, teaching them computer skills and involving them in the work of the Indy Media Center (Garcelon 2006). By 2001, the IMC had 21 members, and in 2003 it had 100 members.

The Argentine site emerged a year later in response to the collapse of the Argentine economy in 2001, when the reports of mainstream media were discredited and suspect (Garcelon 2006). The Argentine site focuses on human rights issues and the history of disappearances and torture. Maria Trijana (quoted in Garcelon 2006), an activist at the IMC, notes that Indy Media was "frontline journalism" during those days and continues to be so. Other sites in Chile, Bolivia, and Colombia followed over the next few years.

Most of the Latin American IMC home pages are organized both thematically and by movements, key among them being movements of workers, peasants, women, indigenous people, and Afro-Latin Americans. Gender, race, and sexuality are emphasized as themes on the sites as well as in the central stories, which include stories on abortion (which is still illegal in most Latin American countries), violence against women, indigenous rights, and Afro-Latin rights. The Latin American IMC websites have postings by individuals as well as by movements and NGO activists.

In addition to the feature stories, each of which is embedded with links and audio, video, or photo clips, sites also list local, regional, and global events, along with links to all the 143 IMCs around the world and to other Indy Media projects like radio, satellite TV, video, and archives of postings. It thus links diverse communities in an attempt to build coalitions. All sites are very explicit about their coalition-building consciousness (Keating 2005).

While the sites welcome all kinds of postings, the editorial policy of the Brazilian website serves to illustrate the exceptions. IMC Brazil excludes posts that

- are racist, sexist or have other discriminatory intentions;
- contain personal attacks;
- are any kind of commercial advert;
- promote an election candidate or a political party;
- are against the principals and values of Indy media Brazil. (www.midiain-dependente.org/en/blue/static/policy.shtml accessed August 4, 2008)

The Indy Media movement in Latin America has been a huge success in combining old and new technologies and creating a computer "underground railroad." The digital networks operate in tandem with social networks. Most sites are in Spanish, except the Brazilian one, which is in Portuguese, French, Italian, and Spanish. As noted before, the Bolivian and Peruvian sites are also in Aymara and Quechua. Most of these sites have a translation program. It is through combining old and new technologies and the use of telecenters that the Latin American IMCs have addressed the issues of access and gender imbalance.

For example, in Argentina, where many people do not have access to the Internet and computers, IMCs have developed ways to bring the Internet to poor people by taking computers to them at work and in their neighborhoods (Boido 2003). In one instance, where two young activists were murdered by the military police, the IMC uploaded pictures of the two involved in movement work and showed them in their neighborhood. Long lines formed to see the two activists, and people shed tears and said prayers in front of the computers. This enabled people to see themselves as change agents and makers of history. The IMC in Argentina also enabled people to film their daily experiences in the context of the financial crisis and then put their films up on the website. Besides enabling ordinary people to become active cultural agents, the IMC also engaged them in constructing their own media.

In Brazil, Indy Media uses traditional media such as radio, video, and print to reach the youth in the favelas and on the streets who are not connected to the Web. In particular, Web-based programs are broadcast on Indy Media radio stations, and local-station broadcasts are uploaded on the IMC site (Ortellado 2002).

IMCs in Latin America have also created media centers, or telecenters, that provide computer access and training to poor youth with no access to computers at home. Most young boys, however, use the telecenters for either looking for jobs, playing games, or surfing pornographic sites. The Brazilian government is now planning to build telecenters in fifteen cities in Brazil. But again research shows that they will have to ensure access for women and girls to ensure equality between the genders.

Telecenters, or *telecottages*, were first introduced in Scandinavia in the 1980s as a way to provide Internet access to rural communities. While some were private, others were funded by the state or local governments. The telecenters worked with local social networks to empower the communities rather than individual network users (Qvortrup 1989). The experience of one women's electronic "village hall" in the UK shows that what was most important in the success of the center was the vision of empowering women (Herman 2001). Creating a culture where technology was women friendly, and accessing it was seen as a right of women—and not as a transgressive act—made a huge difference.

Much of the literature on telecenters is about their market potential, about how to make them economically sustainable, and about which kind of telecenter—privately owned, franchise, government supported, or NGO supported—is most viable (e.g., Proenza, Bastidas-Buch, and Montero 2001). Community telecenters, however, should be conceptualized as community infrastructure, like schools and libraries, and not as economic enterprises (Simpson, Daws, and Pini 2004). Economic profitability places demands that are not always viable. Telecenters should focus on issues of the community, should be organized by the community, and should be managed by the community. Telecenters that combine the livelihood of the communities with their local expertise tend to be the most successful (Russell 2004). Many IMCs in Latin America are based on such a community model.

But giving every poor woman access to a computer will not change gender inequality (Escobar 1999). For that to happen, we need to change power relations in real life. The Women's Networking Support Programme uses the Internet for such strategic use.

THE WOMEN'S NETWORKING SUPPORT PROGRAMME

The Women's Networking Support Programme (henceforth the Programme) grew out of the Association for Progressive Communicators (APC). The APC was formed in 1990 by seven media networks from Europe, the United States, Latin America, and Australia; it came into being to provide Internet access to NGOs participating in the Earth Summit in Rio in 1992. Women active in the APC wanted to form a similar network for women active in the women's movement around environmental and developmental issues. The efforts of these women in the APC resulted in the formation of the Programme in 1993 (APC Women's Networking Support Programme 2000). But in addition to creating a women's network, the APC has also worked to transform its own organizational structure to reflect gender balance and gendered programming. At its 2006 annual meeting, APC members elected, for the first time, a woman to chair the organization. In addition, five out of the eight members of the board, who serve three-year terms, are also women and represent regional and geographic diversity. APC, like many other communications organizations, was male dominated but has worked to address issues of gender inequality, not only by supporting a women's program, but also by transforming its own vision and agenda.

Most of the women who started the Programme had some experience with using the Internet as a tool for activism. They developed a network that included individual women, women's organizations, and women's networks around the world to provide a safe, secure place for networking, mentoring, and support. It is a women-only program, and hence all leadership positions are staffed by women. The Programme's first effort was to provide Internet service to the over 30,000 women who attended the Huairou NGO forum in 1995, held in conjunction with the Fourth World Conference on Women in Beijing, described in chapter 2.

Like Indy Media, the Programme was a response both to needs within the women's movement and to the development of the information and communication technologies. The UN's Fourth World Conference on Women in Beijing served as the immediate catalyst for the Programme. Its aim is

- to initiate and implement research activities in the field of gender and information and communication technologies;
- to advance the body of knowledge, understanding, and skills in the field of gender and information and communication technologies by implementing training activities;
- to facilitate access to information resources in the field of gender and information technologies. (www.apcwomen.org/about_wnsp accessed August 4, 2008)

So while Indy Media's focus is on directly enabling people to become news producers and hence cultural creators, the Programme's focus is on research and training. However, as I will show below, the Programme is involved in building new cultures of globalization. The Programme includes women's groups and organizations, as well as individual women from more than twenty countries. I will focus on the Programme's work in Latin America.

Women's communication networks are not a new cultural form in the contemporary women's movements. Feminists have used media networks from the 1960s onward, both as alternatives to mainstream media coverage and as a space to give voice and expression to women (Kidd 2002). Some examples include the news programs Depth News in Asia, Women's Feature Service in New Delhi, and Caribbean Women's Feature. The International Women's Tribune Center started in 1975 in New York City as a clearinghouse of information for and about women from around the world. Isis International began as a communications and information-sharing service in 1974 in Rome. It moved from Rome to Geneva in the 1980s, and ever since the 1990s there have been three Isis offices, in Manila, Philippines; Kampala, Uganda; and Santiago, Chile. It continues to serve as an important feminist communications network.

The feminist media networks and other community media are about cultural empowerment and hence emphasize the process by which they organize the community and the relationship between the media activists and the community (Meadows, Forde, and Foxwell 2002). Hence, media activists engage community members in dialogue, training future media workers and providing local content.

Following the 1995 Huairou conference, the Programme's aim was to provide activists with a means of staying in touch, sharing and exchanging information, training, and developing ideas and proposals for research and advocacy (www.apcwomen.org/node/93, accessed August 4, 2008). The

Programme's structure reflects its agenda. It consists of a Council of Participants that includes all members. A small coordinating team coordinates and manages projects, and raises funds. The Programme is also composed of members active in specific projects at the regional or local level. In addition, the Programme has "working areas" that organize members by areas of interest, such as the Internet and governance. Finally, it has committees for specific tasks such as hiring, evaluation, and fund-raising (www.apc-women.org/about_wnsp accessed August 4, 2008). The Programme's work is supported by private foundations in the United States and Europe and institutional support from women's organizations.

The Programme is a networked organization that is "multicultural, multidirectional, supportive, affective, sharing, and attentive to the needs of its members." It defines its processes and methods of work as "participatory, consultative, inclusive, egalitarian, flexible and evolving." "Dignity, respect, honor, and security" for each member are part of the Programme's work ethic. As its self-definitions suggest, the Programme takes process seriously. The structure is deliberately flexible, in order to meet the needs of its members and the changing nature of technologies and global contexts. (www.apcwomen.org/about_wnsp accessed August 4, 2008).

The majority of the Programme's members are middle-class European and Third World women and their organizations. Hence, one of the Programme's major efforts is to reach out to poor women, to cross the digital divide using new and old technologies such as radio, posters, and newspapers. Working with the World Association of Community Radio Broadcasters (AMARC) and with Feminist Radio out of Costa Rica, the Programme provides women access to open airwaves for their own programs and ensures the presence of women's voices online through the Women's International Network.

The Programme's main strategy to change unequal gender relations is through shaping global policy around the use of information and communication technologies and, at the local level, organizing women for social change through the use of the Internet:

> Our approach in gender and information and communication technologies involves an understanding of power relations in society. This recognition includes an awareness of the unequal power relations between women and men, north and south, rich and poor, urban and rural, connected and unconnected—in local communities, in sovereign countries, and globally.
>
> WNSP works to transform these relations of inequality, with the full knowledge that information and communication technologies can be used to either exacerbate or transform unequal power relations. Part of this recognition includes an awareness of the limits of information and communication technologies—that in and of themselves, information and communication technologies cannot create gender equality, or end poverty, but that they can be tools for social action and

positive social change. (www.apcwomen.org/about_wnsp accessed August 4, 2008)

As training is its primary activity, I turn attention to the tool kit *Women in Sync (APC WNSP1, APC WNSP2, and APC WNSP3 2000)*, which the Programme produced. It is a collection of stories and experiences of the women and organizations that have become part of the Programme's network, presented in three parts that comprise lessons learned and challenges faced by women's organizations engaged in using communication technologies as a tool for social change. It also serves as a training manual.

I focus on how the Programme's member organizations have worked with women in Latin America to bring about social change (APC WNSP 3 2000). *Women in Sync* emphasizes the importance of the strong women's movement in Latin America in enabling the success of the Internet strategy and creating new global cultures. Various progressive Internet networks that were involved in the APCs in Ecuador, Brazil, Argentina, Mexico, Colombia, Nicaragua, and Uruguay took the lead in promoting the creation of a women's organizations network so women could access information and prepare for the Fourth World Conference on Women in Beijing in 1995. Among the chief initiators of the women's network in Latin America was the Agencia Latinoamericana de Información (Latin American Information Agency; ALAI).

The ALAI was formed in 1977 to promote democratic participation of social movements in Latin American society. It was established as a network to facilitate information sharing among social movements in Latin America, and it remains an important source for social-movement information. In addition to alternative media and journalists, there are many grassroots organizations, women's groups, and academics who are part of the network and contribute to it routinely.

Internet resources enabled the ALAI to flourish as it facilitated faster and more effective communication among its members (Burch 1998). For many academic and social-movement organizations, the ALAI was the only way to communicate with others across borders. And because the Internet was primarily introduced through the institutional arena in Latin America, it enabled the development of collective Internet spaces for collective action—as opposed to the individual consumption and chat use that developed in North America and Europe, where it was introduced to the individual consumer. This has further facilitated the use of cyberspace for social transformation in a region with a rich history of women's movements.

In 1989, to support gender equality, the ALAI established the Area Mujeres (the Women's Programme). This has become an important avenue for women's movements and feminists from diverse backgrounds in Latin America to use in sharing important proposals and strategies. The ALAI also provides training and counseling to establish electronic networks for women's groups. For example, in collaboration with the Programme, it has helped the Afro-Caribbean and Afro-Latin American women's movements develop electronic networks. Because the ALAI works with women's, peasants', and indigenous movements and other human rights struggles, it also serves to bring these movements together through its electronic work. For example, the Area Mujeres has begun to work in rural areas with indigenous women and peasants.

The ALAI has also been promoting advocacy in the region for a right to communicate with a gender focus, that is, inclusion of women's voices and concerns (Burch 1998). It was one of the first networks to promote Spanish- and Portuguese-language websites in the predominantly English cyberspace. Today many websites also have indigenous languages such as Quechua and Aymara, as indicated above.

In preparation for the UN's Fourth World Conference on Women in Beijing, the Area Mujeres collaborated with the Programme to establish more systematic access to the Internet for women's networks in Latin America. The use of the Internet spread rapidly because of the relative unity of language, the strong women's movements in the region, and its relatively easy availability in Latin America compared to other regions in the South.

The main goals of the electronic women's network were promoting awareness, training women from a gender perspective, facilitating a flow of information, and developing policies, advocacy, and research. The Area Mujeres regards the Internet as a site of struggle. Given poor women's lack of access to computers, one of its most important strategies has been to repackage cyber information into radio and print information and make it available to women who lack access to the Internet.

In Mexico, Laneta (slang for "truth") began as a node of APC providing Internet service to civil society organizations, NGOs, and activists. Laneta began promoting the use of the Internet for the women's movement in 1993, and through its work *Modemmujer* began in Mexico in 1995 as a way of gathering an e-mail list of women attending the conference in Beijing. The preparations for the 1995 Beijing conference helped in regional consolidation.

Laneta linked organizations and networks electronically to the Beijing conference by publishing daily bulletins. Three activists in Beijing sent daily reports to the *Modemmujer* site in Mexico City, which then broadcast them to 400 others that, through fax, local newspapers, and community radio, extended the reach even further. *Modemmujer* also provided a reverse information flow, with women in China learning about women in Mexico, their issues, and their struggles.

Modemmujer now reaches a thousand women's organizations in Mexico. It primarily uses e-mail, as many women's organizations don't have access to other Web-based services. They also do not flood their members with information, as most women's organizations do not have the capacity, either technical or substantive, to process information overload. So *Modemmujer* synthesizes, and repackages academic and conference material to make it accessible to rural and poor women's organizations. In addition, given the dominance of English on the Internet, an important part of *Modemmujer*'s work is translating materials into Spanish and Portuguese.

On May 28, 1996, the International Day of Action for Women's Health, *Modemmujer* organized a rally and protest against the Mexican state. They held a tribunal in Mexico City in which women recounted their experiences of forced sterilization and malpractice, resulting in maternal and child mortality, as well as other abuses. As a jury of medical and human-rights experts rendered verdicts on these cases, *Modemmujer* communicated them to their Listserv, who in turn relayed them further.

Modemmujer has developed a weeklong training workshop for women's organizations on using the Internet to strategize and network for women's rights, as well as to lobby and advocate on behalf of women. Hence, *Modemmujer* is engaged in articulating a whole new communicative culture, borrowing from *Modemmujer*'s own history of organizing, and from other Latin American countries.

Following the Beijing conference, the Programme collaborated with Area Mujeres in developing telecenters as a means of reaching more women in poor communities in the rural and urban areas. I discuss several of their projects below to convey a sense of the diversity and scope of their reach. They have reached out to indigenous women's groups to enable them to use the Web to weave a "rhizomatic" (Martinez and Turcotte 2003), gender-based fabric of struggle for visibility, as well as against poverty and violence. In Guatemala, the Centro de Communicadoras is a Mayan site where surfers can sign up with women's cooperatives to learn how to make videos or access women's handicrafts produced by women's cooperatives in the rural areas. The sales are handled by women directly, thus facilitating social economies outside the capitalist system.

But working with indigenous communities has not always been easy. For example, in the Andean town of Pastocalle, where most of the small farmers are indigenous or Mestizo, the farmers came in contact with Chasquinet. Chasquinet is an Area Mujeres and Programme-supported Internet network, based in Quito, that provides Internet access to urban and rural poor communities, to give them a voice so that they can influence economic and social policies that shape their daily lives (APC WNSP 3 2000).[11]

The farmers asked Chasquinet for help in dealing with a plague of ants that were attacking their potato crop. They had made several trips to Quito to government agricultural offices but had gotten nowhere. Chasquinet helped them connect, via the Internet, with other farmers, who helped them with their problem. Following this successful interaction, the local farmers decided to build a telecenter with the help of Chasquinet.

Chasquinet worked with women, as is their strategy, and soon the women wanted to declare their region an ecological reserve to prevent a Dutch hotel from building a resort. They used the Internet to successfully lobby the government. The women also got their children to become involved, and the youth developed Web pages about their reserve. Women also used the Internet for e-commerce for their microcredit enterprises.

It was during this time that Chasquinet found out informally from the girls that the boys were using the telecenter to surf pornographic sites. During discussion of the boys' behavior, the Chasquinet trainer learned that many of the girls had been raped by their male relatives. When the trainer discussed this with the women, she learned that many of the women too had been raped. So the trainers used the Net to talk about sexual abuse, healing, and support-group therapies, which most poor women had never accessed before.

The telecenter became a place for women to come and share their stories and gain support from each other. Many women confronted their abusive spouses. This led to frustration among the men, who complained that women were taking over the telecenter. When a new local leader was chosen he shut down the telecenter, despite protests from the youth and women. The women had, however, learned to support themselves, and now they go to Quito every month to use the computers at Chasquinet. Such experiences reveal the importance of working with men and addressing power inequalities in general in order to continue the work of social transformation.

Chasquinet's experiences with the urban poor have been more positive. In Santa Rosa, a coastal town near Quito, women make a living by picking mussels from the local mangroves. They make about thirty dollars a month. Most of them are illiterate and live in poor communities. Their livelihood was threatened when the local mayor decided to stop the mussel picking and sell the mangrove to shrimp farmers.

Chasquinet learned of this and offered to help. They worked with women to design a campaign in which the local women took part. Chasquinet helped women broadcast their situation and target local and international ecological organizations. They carried out the campaign using radio, as well as by publishing articles in local papers. Greenpeace came to their rescue and began to bombard the local mayor's office with mail. The mayor halted the shrimp farming and the women were able to continue with mussel picking. Emboldened by their success, the women developed a telecenter with the help of Chasquinet and, four years later, are still using the telecenter to access the Internet for their local concerns and for training each other.

In Brazil, the Internet Training Program for Brazilian Women's Network, or Rede Mulher de Educacao, an NGO that facilitates the network of women's organizations throughout Brazil, develops popular feminist education services. Ten women from around Brazil attended a training session and took the knowledge they had acquired back to many other women in their communities. For them, the Internet is a "place to locate [themselves] in the world through the collective thought that transforms all human relationships and political action" (Martinez and Turcotte 2003, 282).

The Programme has also collaborated with the International Development Research Centre in Canada to develop telecenters in marginalized urban neighborhoods and rural communities in Latin America. Ecuanex, an APC node in Ecuador, as well as Colonodo in Colombia, worked with local organizations to set up telecenters in Ecuadorian Amazonia and in Nueva Loja; each telecenter is a hub connected to five computer-radio centers in indigenous communities. In Colombia APC WNSP worked with Fedevivienda, a social-housing umbrella organization, to set up neighborhood information units that would enable individuals in organizations to learn communication skills for community development.

After these projects were set up, conflicts arose that demonstrated the need for redistribution of social power connected to larger economic, cultural, and political contexts. In Colombia, where there is a history of popular women's movements, women have developed collective strategies for the allocation of resources through community networks. Hence, the neighborhood information units were run by teams that were entirely made up of women, and the training process was shaped by women's specific realities in the neighborhoods.

In Ecuadorian Amazonia, where there isn't a popular women's movement, the leadership of the telecenters was in the hands of women who were related to indigenous community leaders. These women did not develop programs to address the issues of women in the community as a whole (APC WNSP 3 2000). While most of the Programme's work with Area Mujeres in Latin America consists of using the Internet for building solidarities and collective action, the Programme has also tried to tie the telecenters to economic initiatives, without making economic empowerment the sole issue.

While electronic networks in Latin America have led to communicational spaces for women in the region, the fear is that commercialization of the Internet might lead to some of the same kinds of consumerist and entertainment-focused individual use that one sees in Europe and North America. ALAI tries to address this threat by providing collective spaces to diverse social movements for networking and information sharing; and also by mobilizing for awareness of these threats; developing proposals with a gender focus for national and international meetings; and developing structures, mechanisms, and practices for democratic communication.

RETHINKING CULTURAL GLOBALIZATION

As noted in the beginning of the chapter, the debates on culture and globalization tend to view both culture and globalization in very narrow terms. Scholars of cultural globalization see culture primarily in terms of consumption of music, dance, clothes, and food, and globalization as a contemporary force, emerging in the West. Based on such an understanding, cultural globalization is understood as cultural homogenization, cultural differentiation, or cultural hybridity. Moreover, cultural hybridity or fusions have emphasized the culture of consumption, especially among the middle and upper classes in the Global North and South, and among the new immigrants.

However, when you look at how ordinary women and men are using the new information and communication technologies, culture as meaning making in daily life becomes evident. You see a new culture of globalization taking shape that involves ordinary men and women in a collective effort of cultural citizenship using the new information and communication technologies.

This new culture of globalization embodies hybridities of virtual and geographic communities; of activists across movements and classes; and of accessing technology and using it for social change and, in the process, developing a common culture based on social justice.

The examples of Indy Media and the Programme represent different dimensions of hybridity. Indy Media has focused on enabling educated men and women to become producers of news and stories. The inequalities of region, class, and education have meant that it is primarily based in the United States and Europe among the educated middle and upper classes. But Indy Media has tried to address this inequality of access by sharing hardware and software.

In Latin America, activists have addressed the digital divide by combining the old media technologies of radio and print with the Internet, and also by developing telecenters in poor communities to provide them access to the new technology. Indy Media has not been as successful, however, in bridging the gender gap.

The Programme, as a women-only network, attempts to bridge the gender gap in the new culture of globalization by training women to access and engage new technologies. Its primary aim is to connect women across communities to organize for gender equality and social justice. As the cases of Chasquinet in Bolivia and Ecuanex in Ecuador show, working for gender equality is a complicated process. As the case of Bolivia demonstrates, not including men can undermine women's access. The case in Amazonian Ecuador shows that including women does not guarantee that all women in those communities will be represented. So gender access remains a complex issue that cannot merely be dealt with by addressing women alone, but rather has to incorporate men, without undermining women.

While both Indy Media and the Programme arose in the context of movements, Indy Media arose from street protest, while the Programme emerged in the context of the UN's Fourth World Conference on Women. These differing contexts map onto the differing strategies adopted by these networks. Indy Media represents what can be possible with the radical potential of the information and communication technologies, while the Programme shows what is possible within the current context. Both have developed new structures and mechanisms for building both virtual and on-the-ground or place-based communities. Both highlight the importance of preexisting social networks and social movements in creating a new culture of globalization.

Collective participation, interactivity, and connectivity for cultural citizenship are the elements that are common to both and that define the new culture of globalization. These new cultures have been initiated by educated, middle-class activists from both the North and the South. Hence, an important focus in both Indy Media and the Programme is the politics of relation, or reaching out across boundaries and inequalities to build a common culture. So it is a politics of recognition but also of participation and redistribution of communication resources. Finally, as the Programme notes:

> Technology is culture which like other cultural processes is then subject to negotiation, contestation, and ultimately transformation. In this perspective the issue is not just access to technology but to the creation of knowledge and technology, in definition, making meanings and creating technological culture. (www.apcwomen.org/about_wnsp accessed August 8, 2008)

NOTES

1. The data for this chapter come primarily from the websites of the groups that I discuss, secondary sources, and my own participation in global conferences and gatherings that have focused on gender and information and communication technologies.

2. As Nederveen Pieterse (2004) notes, this historical view is not common among economists and sociologists but is common among historians and anthropologists.

3. Information and communication technologies include phone, fax, Internet, mobile phones, and various Web-based applications such as discussion groups, chat rooms, instant messaging, and Listservs. I use the term *Internet* to refer to all Web-

based applications and as a shorthand for information and communication technologies.

4. "Plugged In" is a collaboration between Stanford University and several poor East Palo Alto communities.

5. Deuze (2003) suggests that the Internet is a useful communicative tool because of its interactivity, hypertextuality, and multimediality.

6. The two terms, *Indy Media* and the *Independent Media Center (IMC)*, are used interchangeably. In general, however, *Indy Media* is used to denote the global movement, while *IMC* is used for a specific, local center.

7. There is some tyranny of the techies, and there have been some government raids—as in Genoa, Italy, in 2003, after the G8 protests, when an IMC site was broken into at night and computers smashed. But they refuse to be concerned with security, and they maintain an open site.

8. "Caravans" are trips made by Indy Media activists from the North to the South to provide computers and other hardware and software.

9. Google and Yahoo! both gave names of their users to the government to be able to operate in China. The Chinese government used these lists to make arrests and curb political activism.

10. "Squat" building refers to a building that has been abandoned and taken over by poor, homeless people.

11. Unless otherwise indicated, all the examples below are from the *Women in Sync*: Toolkit for Electronic Networking (APC WNSP1, APC WNSP2, APC WNSP3 2000).

4

Engendering Globalization, Policies, and the Global Justice Movement

> The truth is that every day, everywhere in the world at every moment, people are solving problems and finding answers to the challenges of making the world a fairer, cleaner and more beautiful place. Stories about those people and their initiatives are the better stories. (Kamp 2006, 41)

I began this book with the aim of telling those better stories, because the stories we tell shape not only our imaginations but also our actions. I reviewed alternatives and possibilities that men and women have constructed as they have engaged various forms of globalizations. Considering the work of these men and women has enabled us to rethink economic, political, and cultural globalizations. Based on their efforts, here I want to reflect on how a gendered lens enables us to develop a better critical globalization studies; more effective policies for economic, political, and cultural globalizations; and a more nuanced global justice movement.

ENGENDERING A CRITICAL GLOBAL STUDIES

Critical globalization studies have been defined in many ways (e.g., Scholte 2000; Appelbaum and Robinson 2005). While the field includes a variety of theoretical and methodological perspectives, all critical globalization studies highlight two factors: "(1) the subversive nature of its thought in relation to the status-quo, and (2) the linkage (actual or attempted) of theory to practice, or the grounding of a critical globalization studies in praxis, in a theoretically-informed practice" (Robinson 2005, 15).

Mittelman (2005) defines a *critical orientation* as one that not only deconstructs existing knowledge but also constructs new knowledge about what is and what ought to exist, on the basis of transformed relations of power. If we take this charge seriously, then a gender lens is crucial to a critical globalization studies, as gender is a key axis of power relations in all societies. I now turn to how the gendered analysis of the previous chapters contributes to critical global studies.

Women and men, poor and middle class, are as intrinsic a part of globalizations as are the TNCs and their managers. They constitute it even as globalizations shape and limit their possibilities. The cases in the preceding chapters show how men and women, nevertheless, interrogate and rethink globalizations through gendered and situated agencies. Situated or restricted agency does not imply a lack of autonomy, an absence of judgment, or a lack of the capability of agency (Peters 2003). Rather, it demonstrates the innovative and creative ways in which women and men act despite the constraints.

This way of theorizing globalizations moves beyond the binary of globalization from above and globalization from below, which still dominates much writing on globalizations (e.g., Brecher, Costello, and Smith 2000; Falk 2000; Waterman 2002). The binary view of globalizations assumes that there is one center of globalization, namely, the West, and that everything else is a defensive response to that center (McDonald 2006). In emphasizing old intellectual frameworks of social theory, we miss the emerging forms of action and processes in other parts of the world.

More specifically, economic restructuring has increased corporate as well as noncorporate cross-border trade among countries. While most of the focus in the globalization literature has been on formal trade, it is imperative that other forms of cross-border trade be studied more carefully. For in the case of Africa, and perhaps other parts of the world as well, it is the cross-border trade carried out by women that provides food security for the poor throughout the continent. It is trade conducted by women that helps to address the needs of local populations where it is conducted.

A gender lens is particularly necessary here, as the organization of the cross-border trade is deeply gendered, with men represented heavily in the more capital-intensive and more profitable sectors, while women are concentrated in food and other consumer-items trade, and comprise the majority of traders. Despite their concentration in more vulnerable sectors, cross-border trade enables women to lift their families out of poverty, providing security of housing, income, education, and health, as well as empowering women to become decision makers in the household and the community. Hence, it represents an important economic opportunity for women in the era of globalization.

Politically, globalizations have opened up new spaces for new actors to become involved in shaping the gendered processes of globalization. Women's transnational politics has been central in shaping global political practices. As I showed in chapter 2, global politics can be defined as feminist politics in terms of its perspective, organization, and strategies. More specifically, women's experiences of transnational activism around the UN conferences enabled them to develop an intersectional analysis and a transversal politics, or "solidarities of difference." This politics meant developing transnational, networked organizations based on feminist principles of informal and horizontal linkages. Such intersectional or transversal politics has come to define global politics.

Women's transnational activism, however, is not limited to the UN conferences. As I have shown, there are also grassroots women's transnational networks. These networks have formulated strategies of local-local partnerships and global learning academies that have influenced global movements. Taken as a whole, women's transnational activism has been influential in shaping global politics, both in mainstreaming gender concerns and in contributing to organizational and strategic innovations.

In the cultural realm, there are several important practices emerging as a result of the new information and communications technologies. First, there have been new conceptual and practical articulations of cyberpower and cyberfeminism. In the initial euphoria, feminists saw cyberpower and cyberfeminism as panaceas that would revolutionize cultural and political practices. However, these early formulations were about what individuals who have access to computers and the Internet can accomplish in terms of playing with multiple identities, such as cyborgs, and feeling empowered by creating new cultural products, such as zines and blogs.

This initial discourse led to concerns over the digital divide, especially in the Global South. However, there have been innovative, collective efforts that have led to opportunities for people without access to personal computers to engage in cultural citizenship. Through telecenters, the repackaging of Web-based information, training, and other exchange efforts, poor women and men who do not own personal computers have been able to participate in the information age, and to articulate their sense of a common culture.

Hence, cyberpower and cyberfeminism have been redefined as collective connections, or relationships between virtual and place-based power and feminisms, which allow more men and women to have that power and use it to shape their culture, as reflected by their realities and expectations. Furthermore, these new cultures of globalization also develop solidarities across borders for both political and cultural work, which is carried out under new rules of engagement that highlight horizontal linkages and participatory methods. Thus, the action, processes, and organizations of cultural globalization have a new grammar (e.g., Castells 2000; McDonald 2006). It has changed the way people imagine culture and politics. Information and communication technologies facilitate not solely a universal imagination, but also plural and multidimensional consciousnesses that can inform policy at various levels.

ENGENDERING GLOBAL AND LOCAL POLICIES

The understanding of globalizations from the point of view of ordinary men and women allows us to rethink current policies and to make specific recommendations.

In the economic realm, due to the dominance of neoliberal policies in most countries, most of the policy literature emphasizes how "informal" trade can be formalized—how governments can regulate it, so they can collect taxes and provide more health and safety guidelines (as a huge part of the trade is in perishable agricultural and food products). Other policy recommendations, also from a neoliberal perspective, focus on immigration, arguing for the relaxation of immigration constraints.

In contrast to the above policies formulated by government agencies and policy analysts, women cross-border traders have different recommendations. First, they want legitimacy and recognition. Women traders argue that governments take their trading activity just as seriously as corporate trade. Thus, cross-border traders should receive tax breaks, and their goods should be tax-exempt, as is the case for corporate trade. Such recognition will cut down on corruption and bribery and make trade more profitable for the traders, and eventually for the economies of all countries in the region (Plunkett and Stryker 2002).

In terms of facilitating their travel across borders, women traders ought to have multientry trading permits rather than having to get tourist visas, which cost more (Cheater 1998; Cheater and Gaidzanwa 1996). Some NGOs have even recommended that a badge be given to traders in western Africa for easy and hassle-free travel across borders (CORN and AFSC 2004b). This would be particularly easy now that most countries have signed regional free-trade agreements that could facilitate travel across borders for women.

Scholars and NGOs working with women cross-border traders also have other specific policy recommendations. For example, women cross-border traders require better credit, infrastructure, and transportation, and more access to information and knowledge about markets (e.g., Morris and Saul 2005; Cheater 1998; Peberdy and Crush 1998; CORN and AFSC 2004b).

In the political realm, the activist perspective suggests important policy guidelines for global gender equity. Gender mainstreaming as policy is contentious, is applied differentially across institutions and countries, and is often focused only on employment and on violence against women (Walby 2005). Gender mainstreaming is based on multiple assumptions of gender equality: the assumption of sameness, which leads to tinkering with extant policies; acknowledged differences, which assumption results in tailoring policies to accommodate gender differences; and transformation, which challenges existing gender policies to impact both men and women (Rees 2005). The globalization of gender mainstreaming as policy and practice has been uneven and has often involved transfer of practices from the North to the South.

But grassroots women's transnational activism suggests that policies that forge ongoing partnerships with local authorities tend to ensure that poor women and men have access to decision making in local power structures, as well as access to local resources. Such partnerships, rooted in local realities and based on capacity building, can begin to engage women and men in what have been called "grounded utopias" (Mittelman 2005) or "real utopias" (Wright 2006).

In the cultural realm, government policies have focused on the digital divide and access, rather than on how women and men can use these technologies for cultural empowerment and transformation. As the experiences of the Indy Media movement and the Women's Networking Support Programme show, when the objective of information and communication technologies is well articulated, it is easy to think of ways to address issues of access. Instituting a policy that makes telecenters part of the community infrastructure, like libraries and schools, is one way of addressing issues of access.

Education and training for use of such technologies also makes cultural citizenship possible. Hence, policies around information and communication technologies should not focus so much on the digital divide per se. Rather, the issue is one of linking access to technologies with other services, such as education, health, and training for livelihoods, taking into consideration community needs and networks. Most importantly, the policies need to recognize the right of citizens to be knowledge producers and cultural creators.

Beyond policy implications, rethinking globalization from the perspective of ordinary men and women also contributes to the global justice movement.

ENGENDERING THE GLOBAL JUSTICE MOVEMENT

Susan George, a scholar-activist in the global justice movement, asks:

> What should be the role and responsibilities of academia and the intellectuals in the global justice movement? Can we, together, create a body of work

relevant to the theme of a critical globalization studies? Can we help this movement attain its goals through the tools of scholarship? Can we help it to analyze the present structures of injustice, formulate workable proposals for change, devise the best strategies to convince ordinary people and decision-makers of their relevance, and change the rapport de forces? (George 2005, 3)

Her answer, and mine, is yes, we can. Feminists, among other scholar-activists, have been doing this for quite some time now. Here, I show how women, as shapers of various globalizations, can contribute to the global justice movement.

The politics of the global justice movement around economic restructuring has focused on anticorporate, anti-WTO, and anti-IMF protests. While such protests and mobilizations have been important in delegitimizing economic restructuring, they have not led to real economic well-being for the majority of the world's poor. By contrast, women traders have shown what they have been able to achieve for themselves, their families, and their communities by using the opportunities made available by economic restructuring.

Women cross-border traders thus focus on organizing financial, marketing, production, transportation, accommodation, and communication networks among themselves, and with others in the community. Financial networks would relieve the credit pressure from family or kin, who are currently the primary source of credit for most traders. Marketing networks would avoid saturation and competition by developing new markets for sustainable trade. Production networks would help women produce goods for sale, while cross-border transportation networks would provide safe and guaranteed transportation (an important concern, given the paucity of public transportation in most countries in the Global South).

Networks for accommodation would provide affordable and safe housing, while networks for storage would provide space for goods, so women would not have to sleep with their goods or risk being robbed. Currently, there are no warehouses available in reasonable places or at reasonable prices. Finally, networks for communication would facilitate data collection on new markets and new demands, to avoid excessive competition and poor profits.

Thus, the global justice movement needs to incorporate and highlight strategies that provide viable alternatives to corporate globalization. Among such alternatives are using the openings provided by economic restructuring to develop social economies through producer/consumer cooperatives that can facilitate the economic well-being of workers, traders, and farmers; and state policies that support such economic activities outside the corporate sector.

Such economic alternatives challenge what critical global scholars call "neoliberal governmentality," that is, a policy of creating responsible, private economic subjects whose actions further corporate globalization. This transformation of citizens into economic agents is also evident in the promotion of microcredit programs, a key program advocated by all actors of corporate globalization. One indication of the popularity of these programs is the awarding of the 2006 Nobel Peace prize to Mohammad Yunus, the founder of the Grameen Bank in Bangladesh, which promotes microcredit for poor women.

Culturally, the technologies of globalization create possibilities for politics that enable linkages between virtual and place-based politics for organizing and mobilizing. The various examples discussed in chapter 2 demonstrate the effectiveness of such multiscalar organizing. In all those cases, cyberpower was effective only in conjunction with real power. And in all instances, it was important to organize women and men together, as well as on their own, to ensure gender and social equality.

In the political arena, women's transnational activism has several insights for the global justice movement. Global politics is feminist in terms of its theoretical perspective, organizational forms, practices, and strategies. Women tend to use practices that renegotiate the public/private boundaries, at sites that are mostly local and community based but also, increasingly, transnational. Or women's transnational politics is gendered in terms of its form and content and its relational thinking, and in terms of identity as well as politics of location (Marchand 2003). But what women's politics has also shown is that, in terms of identity, women organize as women in the global justice movement, but men almost never organize as men. It is important that men involved in the global justice movement organize based on feminist masculinities, recognizing the patriarchal dividends they accrue, if we are to transform gender inequality and articulate egalitarian social relations.

Finally, women's transnational activism shows that the global justice movement takes gender seriously only when women put it on the agenda. Part of this stems from the fact that men have not yet begun to organize as men and recognize the ways in which politics is gendered. Engendering politics should be about more than including women and their issues; it is for everyone, so that all can recognize how gender operates in all power relations and how people, as gendered beings, need to think of what gender relations ought to be.

These are only some of the possibilities that come to light when we use a gendered lens to rethink globalizations. There is a world of possibilities for social justice, to be discovered and imagined as we continue to engage both gender and globalizations seriously and creatively.

Bibliography

Abu-Lughod, Janet. 1989. *Before European Hegemony: The World System A.D. 1250–1350*. New York: Oxford University Press.

Acker, Joan. 2005. *Class Questions: Feminist Answers*. Lanham, MD: Rowman & Littlefield.

———. 2004. "Gender, Capitalism, and Globalization." *Critical Sociology* 30 (1): 17–41.

Akinboade, Oludele Akinloye. 2005. "A Review of Women, Poverty, and Informal Trade Issues in East and Southern Africa." *International Social Science Journal* 57 (184): 255–75.

Alkalimat, Abdul, and Kate Williams. 2001. "Social Capital and Cyberpower in the African-American Community: A Case Study of a Community Technology Centre in the Dual City." In *Community Informatics: Shaping Computer-Mediated Social Relations*, edited by Leigh Keeble and Brian D. Loader, 177–204. New York: Routledge.

Anzaldua, Gloria. 1990. *Borderlands/La Frontera: The New Mestiza*. San Francisco: Aunt Lute Books.

APC WNSP 1 2000. *Putting Beijing Online: Women Woring in ICT*. www.apcwomen .org/netsupport/sync/toolkit1.pdf, accessed August 4, 2008.

APC WNSP 2 2000. *Networking for Change: The APCWNSP's First Eight Years*. www .apcwomen.org/netsupport/sync/toolkit2.pdf, accessed August 4, 2008.

APC WNSP 3 2000. *Acting Locally, Connecting Globally: Stories From the Regions*. www .apcwomen.org/netsupport/sync/toolkit3.pdf, accessed August 4, 2008.

Appadurai, Arjun. 2002. "Deep Democracy: Urban Governmentality and the Horizon of Politics." *Public Culture* 14 (1): 21–47.

———. 2000. "Grassroots Globalization and the Research Imagination." *Public Culture* 12 (1): 1–19.

———. 1996. *Modernity at Large: Cultural Dimensions of Globalization*. Minneapolis: University of Minnesota Press.

Appelbaum, Richard P., and William I. Robinson, eds. 2005. *Critical Globalization Studies*. New York: Routledge.

Archibugi, D, ed. 2003. *Debating Cosmopolitics*. London: Verso.

Arizpe, Lourdes. 1998. "Freedom to Create: Women's Agenda for Cyberspace." In *Women@Internet: Creating New Cultures in Cyberspace*, edited by Wendy Harcourt, xii–xvi. London: Zed Books.

Asiedu, Christobel. 2006. "Using Information and Communication Technologies for Gender and Development in Africa." Ph.D. dissertation, University of Illinois.

Atton, Chris. 2004. *An Alternative Internet*. Edinburgh: Edinburgh University Press.

———. 2001. "Approaching Alternative Media: Theory and Methodology." Paper presented at the Our Media, Not Theirs I conference. Washington, DC.

Basu, Amrita, and Inderpal Grewal, eds. 2001. Special Issue on Globalization and Gender, *Signs* 26, no. 4 (Summer).

Baud, M., and R. Rutten, eds. 2005. *Popular Intellectuals and Social Movements: Framing Protest in Asia, Africa, and Latin America*. New York: Cambridge University Press.

Belausteguigoitia Rius, Marisa. 1998. "Crossing Borders: From Crystal Slippers to Tennis Shoes." In *Women@Internet: Creating New Cultures in Cyberspace*, edited by Wendy Harcourt, 23–30. London: Zed Books.

Beneria, Lourdes. 2003. *Economics as if People Mattered*. London: Routledge.

Beneria, Lourdes, and Shelley Feldman. 1992. *Unequal Burden: Economic Crises, Persistent Poverty, and Women's Work*. Boulder, CO: Westview.

Bhagwati, Jagdish. 2004. *In Defense of Globalization*. New York: Oxford University Press.

Boido, Pablo. 2003. "IMC in Argentina." Paper presented at the Our Media, Not Theirs III conference, Barranquilla, Colombia.

Boserup, Ester. 1970. *Woman's Role in Economic Development*. New York: St. Martin's.

Brah, Avtar, Mary Hickman, and Mairtin Mac an Ghaill, eds. 1999. *Global Futures: Migration, Environment, and Globalization*. London: Macmillan Press.

Bray-Crawford, Kekula. 1998. "The Ho'okele Netwarriors in the Liquid Continent." In *Women@Internet: Creating New Cultures in Cyberspace*, edited by Wendy Harcourt, 162–72. London: Zed Books.

Brecher, Jeremy, Tim Costello, and Brendan Smith. 2000. *Globalization from Below*. Cambridge, MA: South End Press.

Bunch, Charlotte, and Niamh Reilly. 1994. *Demanding Accountability: The Global Campaign and Vienna Tribunal for Women's Human Rights*. New Brunswick: Center for Women's Global Leadership.

Burbach, R. 2001. *Globalization and Postmodern Politics: From Zapatistas to Hi-tech Robber Barons*. London: Pluto Press.

Burch, Sally. 1998. "ALAI: A Latin American Experience in Social Networking." In *Women@Internet: Creating New Cultures in Cyberspace*, edited by Wendy Harcourt, 197–205. London: Zed Books.

Burton, Barbara. 2004. "Transmigration of Rights: Women, Movement, and the Grassroots in Latin American and Caribbean Communities." *Development and Change* 35 (4): 773–98.

Butler, Judith. 1999. *Gender Trouble*. London: Routledge.

Cagatay, Nilufer. 2003. "Gender Budgets and Beyond: Feminist Fiscal Policy in the Context of Globalization." In *Women Reinventing Globalization*, edited by Joanna Kerr and Caroline Sweetman, 15–24. Oxford: Oxfam.

Calhoun, Craig. 2002. "Imagining Solidarity: Cosmopolitanism, Constitutional Patriotism, and the Public Sphere." *Public Culture* 14 (1): 147–71.

Carr, Marilyn, and Martha Chen. 2002. "Globalization and the Informal Economy: How Global Trade and Investment Impact on the Working Poor." Employment Sector Working Paper on the Informal Economy No. 2002/1, International Labour Organization, Geneva.

Castells, M. 2000. "Globalization and Identity in the Network Society: A Rejoinder to Calhoun, Lyon and Touraine." *Prometheus* 4: 109–23.

———. 1999. *Information Technology, Globalization and Social Development*. Geneva: United Nations Institute for Social Development.

Castells, Manuel, and Alejandro Portes. 1989. "World Underneath: The Origins, Dynamics, and Effects of the Informal Economy." In *The Informal Economy: Studies in Advanced and Less Advanced Developed Countries*, edited by Alejandro Portes, Manuel Castells, and Lauren A. Benton, 11–40. Baltimore, MD: The Johns Hopkins University Press.

Cavanagh, John, and Jerry Mander, eds. 2004. *Alternatives to Economic Globalization: A Better World is Possible*. San Francisco: Berrett-Koehler.

Chaney, David. 2002. "Cosmopolitan Art and Cultural Citizenship." *Theory, Culture, and Society* 19 (1–2): 157–74.

Chang, Grace. 2000. *Disposable Domestics: Immigrant Women Workers in the Global Economy*. Cambridge, MA: South End Press.

Chang, K., and L. H. M. Ling. 2000. "Globalization and Its Intimate Other: Filipina Domestic Workers in Hong Kong." In *Gender and Global Restructuring: Sightings, Sites, and Resistances*, edited by Marianne H. Marchand and Anne Sisson Runyan, 27–43. London: Routledge.

Chari, Unity. 2004. "Informal Cross-Border Trade and Gender." Paper presented at the Workshop on Sustainable Development through Trade, Harare, Zimbabwe, February.

Chase-Dunn, Christopher. 1998. *Global Formation: Structures of the World-Economy*. 2nd ed. Lanham, MD: Rowman & Littlefield.

Chase-Dunn, Christopher, and Barry Gills. 2005. "Waves of Globalization and Resistance in the Capitalist World-System: Social Movements and Critical Globalization Studies." In *Critical Globalization Studies*, edited by Richard P. Appelbaum and William I. Robinson, 45–54. New York: Routledge.

Chatterjee, Bela Bonita. 2002. "Razorgirls and Cyberdykes: Tracing Cyberfeminism and Thoughts on Its Use in a Legal Context." *International Journal of Sexuality and Gender Studies* 7 (2/3): 197–213.

Cheah Pheng and Bruce Robbins (editors). 1998. *Cosmopolitics: Thinking and Feeling Beyod the Nation*. Mineapolis: University of Minnesota Press.

Cheater, Angela. 1998. "Transcending the State? Gender and Borderline Constructions of Citizenship in Zimbabwe." In *Border Identities: Nation and State at International Frontiers*, edited by Thomas Wilson and Hastings Donnan, 191–214. Cambridge, UK: Cambridge University Press.

Cheater, Angela, and R. B. Gaidzanwa. 1996. "Citizenship in Neo-patrilineal States: Gender and Mobility in Southern Africa." *Journal of Southern African Studies* 22 (2): 189–200.

Chen, Martha Alter. 2001. "Women in the Informal Sector: A Global Picture, the Global Movement." *SAIS Review* 21, no. 1 (Winter–Spring): 71–82.

Chow, Esther. 2003. "Gender Matters: Studying Globalization and Social Change in the 21st Century." *International Sociology* 18 (3): 443–60.

Commission on the Status of Women. www.un.org/womenwatch/daw/csw.

Community Organizations' Regional Network (CORN) and American Friends Service Committee (AFSC). 2004a. *Sustainable Livelihood and Economic Development Through Trade. Fact Sheet 1.* www.zeroregional.com/publications/Factsheets%20Dec/Fact%20Sheet%20Folder.pdf, accessed August 8, 2008.

———. 2004b. *Common Problems Relating to Cross Border Trade.* Fact Sheet 2. www.zeroregional.com/publications/Factsheets%20Dec/Fact%20Sheet%20Folder.pdf, accessed August 8, 2008

———. 2004c. *The Southern African Development Community.* Fact Sheet 3. www.zeroregional.com/publications/Factsheets%20Dec/Fact%20Sheet%20Folder.pdf, accessed August 8, 2008.

———. 2004d. *Testimonies from Cross Border Traders in the SADC Region.* Fact Sheet 4. www.zeroregional.com/publications/Factsheets%20Dec/Fact%20Sheet%20Folder.pdf, accessed August 8, 2008.

Connell, Robert. 2004. "The Role of Men and Boys in Achieving Gender Equality." Panel discussion, Commission on Status of Women meeting, New York, March 2.

Cotler, Angelina. 2005. "Microenterprise in Peru." Ph.D. dissertation, University of Illinois.

Couldry, Nick. 2003. "Beyond the Hall of Mirrors? Some Theoretical Reflections on the Global Contestations of Media Power." In *Contesting Media Power: Alternative Media in a Networked World*, edited by Nick Couldry and James Curran, 39–54. Lanham, MD: Rowman & Littlefield.

Couldry, Nick, and James Curran, eds. 2003. *Contesting Media Power: Alternative Media in a Networked World.* Lanham, MD: Rowman & Littlefield.

Cox, Kevin R., ed. 1997. *Spaces of Globalization: Reasserting the Power of the Local.* New York: Guilford Press.

Coyer, Kate. 2005a. "Where the Hyper Local and the Hyper Global Meet: Case Study of Indymedia Radio." *Westminster Papers in Communication and Culture* 2 (1): 30–50.

———. 2005b. "If It Leads It Bleeds: The Participatory Newsmaking of the Independent Media Center." In *Global Activism, Global Media*, edited by Wilma de Jong, Martin Shaw, and Neil Stammers, 165–78. London: Pluto Press.

Darkwah, Akosua. 2007. "Making Hay While the Sun Shines: Ghanaian Female Traders and Their Insertion into the Global Economy." In *The Gender of Globalization: Women Navigating Cultural and Economic Marginalities*, edited by Nandini Gunewardena and Ann Kingsolver. Albuquerque, NM: SAR Press.

———. 2002. "Going Global: Ghanaian Female Transnational Traders in an Era of Globalization." Ph.D. dissertation, University of Wisconsin, Madison.

Day, Richard. 2004. "From Hegemony to Affinity: The Political Logic of the Newest Social Movements." *Cultural Studies* 18 (5): 716–48.

de Sousa Santos, Boaventura. 2006. *The Rise of the Global Left: The World Social Forum and Beyond.* London: Zed Books.

Dean, Jodi. 2002. *Publicity's Secret: How Technoculture Capitalizes on Democracy.* Ithaca, NY: Cornell University Press.

Dejene, Yeshiareg. 2001. *Women's Cross-Border Trade in West Africa.* USAID Women In Development Technical Assistance (WIDTech) Project. Washington DC.

Delgadillo, Karin, Ricardo Gómez, and Klaus Stoll. 2002. *Community Telecentres for Development: Lessons Learned from Latin America and the Caribbean.* Ottawa, Canada: IDRC and CDRI.

Della Porta, Donatella, Massamiliano Andretta, Lorenzo Mosca, and Herbert Reiter. 2006. *Globalization From Below: Transnational Activists and Protest Networks.* Minneapolis: University of Minnesota Press.

Denis, Ann. 2003. "Globalization, Women, and (In)Equity in the South: Constraints and Resistance in Barbados." *International Sociology* 18 (3): 491–512.

Denis, Ann, and Michele Ollivier. 2003. "How Wired Are Canadian Women? The Intersections of Gender, Class, and Language in Information Technologies." In *Out of the Ivory Tower: Feminist Research for Social Change,* edited by Andrea Martinez and Meryn Stuart, 251–69. Toronto: Sumac Press.

Desai, Manisha. 2005. "Transnationalism: The Face of Feminist Politics Post-Beijing." *International Social Science Journal* 57 (2): 319–30.

———. 2002. "Transnational Solidarity: Women's Agency, Structural Adjustment and Globalization." In *Globalization and Women's Activism: Linking Local Struggles to Transnational Politics,* edited by N. Naples and M. Desai, 15–33. New York: Routledge.

———. 1999. "From Vienna to Beijing: Women's Human Rights Activism and the Human Rights Community." In *Debating Human Rights: Critical Essays from the United States and Asia,* edited by Peter Van Ness, 184–96. New York: Routledge.

———. 1997. "Constructing/Deconstructing 'Women': Reflections from the Contemporary Women's Movement in India." In *Feminism and the New Democracy: Resisting the Political,* edited by Jodi Dean, 110–23. Newbury Park, CA: Sage.

———. 1996. "'If Peasants Build Their Own Dams, What Will the State Have Left to Do?' The Practices of a New Social Movement in India." *Research in Social Movements, Conflict, and Change* 19: 203–18.

Deuze, Mark. 2003. "The Internet and its Journalisms: Considering the Consequences of Different Types of News Media Online." *New Media and Society* 5 (20): 203–30.

Diani, Mario. 2000. "Social Movement Networks Virtual and Real." *Information, Communication and Society* 3 (3): 386–401.

Dodson, Belinda. 1998. *Women on the Move: Gender and Cross-Border Migration to South Africa.* South African Migration Policy Series Paper No. 9, at www.queensu.ca/samp/, accessed April 6, 2006.

Downing, John. 2005. "Activist Media, Civil Society, and Social Movements." In *Global Activism, Global Media,* edited by Wilma de Jong, Martin Shaw, and Neil Stammers, 149–64. London: Pluto Press.

———. 2003. "The Independent Media Center Movement and the Anarchist Socialist Tradition." In *Contesting Media Power: Alternative Media in a Networked World,* edited by Nick Couldry and James Curran, 243–57. Lanham, MD: Rowman & Littlefield.

Ehrenreich, Barbara, and Arlie Russell Hochschild. 2002. *Global Woman: Nannies, Maids, and Sex Workers in the New Economy.* New York: Henry Holt.

Elson, Diane. 1994. "Uneven Development and the Textiles and Clothing Industry." In *Capitalism and Development,* edited by Leslie Sklair, 189–210. London: Routledge.

Eschle, Catherine. 2005. "'Skeleton Women': Feminism and the Antiglobalization Movement." *Signs* 30 (31): 1741–69.

———. 2001. *Democracy, Globalization and Social Movements.* Boulder, CO: Westview.

Escobar, Arturo. 1999. "Gender, Place, and Networks: A Political Ecology of Cyberculture." In *Women@Internet: Creating New Cultures in Cyberspace,* edited by Wendy Harcourt, 31–54. London: Zed Books.

Everett, Anna. 2004. "On Cyberfeminism and Cyberwomanism: High-Tech Mediations of Feminism's Discontents." *Signs* 30 (1): 1278–86.

Falk, Richard A. 2000. *Human Rights Horizons: The Pursuit of Justice in a Globalizing World.* New York: Routledge.

———. 1999. *Predatory Globalization: A Critique.* Malden, MA: Blackwell.

Featherstone, Mike, ed. 1990. *Global Culture: Nationalism, Globalization and Modernity.* London: Sage.

Feminist Dialogues. (2007). http://feministdialogues.isiswomen.org/.

———. 2007. *Transforming Democracy: Feminist Vision and Strategies: Global Report.* Manila: Isis.

———. 2005. *Radical Democracy: Global Report.* Manila: Isis.

Ferree, Myra Marx, and Aili Mari Tripp. 2006. *Global Feminism: Transnational Women's Activism, Organizing, and Human Rights.* New York: New York University Press.

Flynn, Donna K. 1997. "'We are the Border': Identity, Exchange, and the State along the Bénin-Nigeria Border." *American Ethnologist* 24 (2): 311–30.

Fontana, M., S. Joekes, and R. Masika. 1998. *Global Trade Expansion and Liberalization: Gender Issues and Impacts.* Bridge Briefings on Development and Gender 42. Brighton, UK: Institute of Development Studies.

Freeman, Carla. 2001. "Is Local: Global as Feminine: Masculine? Rethinking the Gender of Globalization." *Signs* 26 (4): 1007–33.

Friedman, Thomas L. 2005. *The World is Flat: A Brief History of the Twenty-First Century.* New York: Picador.

Fuentes, Annette, and Barbara Ehrenreich. 1983. *Women in the Global Economy.* Boston, MA: South End Press.

Fuentes, Martha, and Joseph Straubhaar. 2001. *Improving Public Internet Access in Brazil: Moving Beyond Connectivity.* Report for School of the Future. São Paulo, Brazil: University of São Paulo.

Gaidzanwa, R. B. 1993. "Citizenship, Nationality, Gender and Class in Southern Africa." *Alternatives* 18:39–59.

Gajjala, Radhika, and Annapurna Mamidipudi. 1999. "Cyberfeminism, Technology and International Development." *Gender and Development* 7 (2): 8–16.

Garcelon, Marc. 2006. "The 'Indymedia' Experiment: The Internet as Movement Facilitator Against Institutional Control." *Convergence* 12 (1): 55–82.

George, Susan. 2005. "If You Want To Be Relevant: Advice to the Academic." In *Critical Globalization Studies,* edited by Richard P. Appelbaum and William I. Robinson, 3–10. New York: Routledge.

Gibson, Nigel. 2004 "Africa and Globalization: Marginalization and Resistance." *Journal of African and Asian Studies* 39 (1/2): 1–28.

Giddens, Anthony. 1999. *Runaway World: How Globalization is Reshaping Our Lives.* London: Profile Books.

Gordo, Blanca. 2003. "Overcoming Digital Deprivation." *IT and Society* 1 (5): 166–80.

Gottfried, Heidi. 2004. "Gendering Globalization Discourses." *Critical Sociology* 30 (1): 9–15.

Graham-Gibson, J. K. 1996. *The End of Capitalism (As We Knew It): A Feminist Critique of Political Economy.* Minneapolis: University of Minnesota Press.

Guidry, John A., Michael D. Kennedy, and Mayer N. Zald. 2000. "Globalizations and Social Movements." In *Globalizations and Social Movements: Culture, Power and the Transnational Public Sphere,* edited by John A. Guidry, Michael D. Kennedy, and Mayer N. Zald, 1–43. Ann Arbor: University of Michigan Press.

Hamel, P., H. Lustier-Thaler, J. Nederveen Pieterse, and S. Roseneil, eds. 2001. *Globalization of Social Movements.* New York: Palgrave.

Hanke, Bob. 2005. "For a Political Economy of Indymedia Practice." *Canadian Journal of Communication* 30 (1): 41–64.

Haraway, Donna. 1997. *Modest_Witness@Second_Millennium.FemaleMan©_Meets_ OncoMouse™: Feminism and Technoscience.* New York: Routledge.

Harcourt, Wendy, ed. 1999. *Women@Internet: Creating New Cultures in Cyberspace.* London: Zed Books.

Hardt, Michael, and Antonio Negri. 2004. *Multitude: War and Democracy in the Age of Empire.* New York: Penguin Press.

Harvey, David. 1989. *The Condition of Postmodernity.* Oxford: Blackwell Publishers.

Hashim, Yahya, and Kate Meagher. 1999. *Cross-Border Trade and the Parallel Currency Market: Trade and Finance in the Context of Structural Adjustment; A Case Study from Kano, Nigeria.* Uppsala: Nordiska Afrikainstitutet.

Hawthorne, Susan. 2004. "Wild Politics: Beyond Globalization." *Women Studies International Forum* 727: 243–59.

Hawthorne, Susan, and Renate Klein. 1999. *Cyberfeminism: Connectivity, Critique and Creativity.* North Melbourne, Australia: Spinifex Press.

Hayles, N. Katherine. 1995. "The Life Cycle of Cyborgs: Writing the Posthuman." In *The Cyborg Handbook,* edited by C. H. Gray, 321–35. New York: Routledge.

Hearn, Jeff, and Michael Messner. 2006. "Changing Studies on Men and Masculinities." In *Handbook of Gender and Women's Studies,* edited by Kathy Davis, Mary Evans, and Judith Lorber. London: Sage.

Held, David. 2002. *Globalization/Anti-globalization.* Cambridge, UK: Polity Press.

Herman, C. 2001. "From Visions to Reality: Changing Women's Perspectives at the Village Hall." *ACM SIGCAS Computers and Society* 31 (4): 15–22.

Herndon, S. 2003. Barranquilla Presentation/notes. http://ourmedianetwork.org/ ?q=node/77, accessed August 4, 2008.

Hirst, Paul, and Graham Thompson. 1999. *Globalisation in Question.* Cambridge, UK: Polity Press.

Huairou Commission. www.huairou.org.

———. 2006. "Report to Partners," at www.huairou.org.

———. 2002. "Urban Governance Tool Kit Series," at www.huairou.org.

———. 2000. "Newsletter," at www.huairou.org.

Huntington, Samuel P. 1993. "The Clash of Civilizations?" *Foreign Affairs*, 72(3):

Hyde, Gene. 2002. "Independent Media Centers: Cyber-Subversion and the Alternative Press." *First Monday* 7, no. 4 (April). firstmonday.org/issues/issue7_4/hyde/index.html, accessed April 6, 2006.

Independent Media Center. www.indymedia.org.

International Labour Organization. 1972. *Kenya Mission Report*. Geneva: ILO Publications.

Jorge, Sonia N. 2000. "Gender Perspectives on Telecenters." Communications: Universal Access and Community Telecenters, Telecom Development Symposium, ITU-Telecom Americas 2000, April 11.

Kabeer, Naila. 2004. "Globalisation, Labour Standards, and Women's Rights: Dilemmas of (In)Action in an Interdependent World." *Feminist Economics* 10 (1): 3–35.

Kahn, Richard, and Douglas Kellner. 2004. "New Media and Internet Activism: From the Battle of Seattle to Blogging." *New Media and Society* 16 (1): 87–95.

Kallungia, Sam K. 2001. *Impact of Informal Cross Border Trade in Eastern and Southern Africa*. Lusaka: COMESA, Regional Integration Research Network.

Kamp, Jurriaan. 2006. "What the World Needs Now Are Better Stories." *Ode Magazine*. www.odemagazine.com/doc/32/what_the_world_needs_now_are_better_stories, accessed June 10, 2006.

Kardam, Nuket. 2004. "The Emerging Global Gender Equality Regime from Neoliberal and Constructivist Perspectives." *International Feminist Journal of Politics* 6 (1): 95–109.

Kasic, Biljana. 2004. "Feminist Cross Mainstreaming within East-West Mapping: A Post-Socialist Perspective." *European Journal of Women's Studies* 11 (4): 473–85.

Keane, John. 2003. *Global Civil Society?(* Contemporary Political Theory. Cambridge, UK: Cambridge University Press.

Keating, Cricket. 2005. "Building Coalitional Consciousness." *NWSA Journal* 17 (2): 86–103.

Keck, Margaret E., and Kathryn Sikkink. 1998. *Activists Beyond Borders: Advocacy Networks in International Politics*. Ithaca, NY: Cornell University Press.

Kember, Sara. 2003. *Cyberfeminism and Artificial Life*. New York: Routledge.

Kerr, Joanna, and Caroline Sweetman, eds. 2003. *Women Reinventing Globalisation*. Oxford: Oxfam.

Khagram, Sanjeev, James Riker, and Kathryn Sikkink. 2002. *Restructuring World Politics: Transnational Social Movements, Networks, and Norms*. Minneapolis: University of Minnesota Press.

Kidd, Dorothy. 2003. "Carnival and Commons: The Global IMC Network." Paper presented at the Our Media, Not Theirs III conference, Barranquilla, Colombia.

———. 2002. "Which Would You Rather: Seattle or Porto Alegre?" Paper presented at the Our Media, Not Theirs II conference, Barcelona, Spain.

Kofman, Eleonore. 2004. "Gendered Global Migrations." *International Feminist Journal of Politics* 6 (4): 643–65.

Koggel, Christine. 2003. "Globalization and Women's Paid Work: Expanding Freedom?" *Feminist Economics* 9 (2–3): 163–83.

Kvasny, Lynette. 2006. "Cultural (Re)production of Digital Inequality in a US Community Technology Initiative." *Information, Communication and Society* 9 (2): 160–81.

———. 2003. "Triple Jeopardy: Race, Gender and Class Politics of Women in Technology." Paper presented at the SIGMIS conference, Philadelphia, April 10–12.

Kymlicka, Will. 1996. *Multicultural Citizenship: A Liberal Theory of Minority Rights.* Oxford: Oxford University Press.

Lang, James L., and Geoffrey D. Prewitt. 2001. "Men's Involvement in Gender Mainstreaming: A Case Study of the United Nations." Paper presented at the Working with Men to End Gender Violence conference, Bellagio, Italy, October 8–12.

Leavitt, Jacqueline. 2000. *Grassroots Women's Collectives [sic] Roles in Post-Disaster Effort.* New York: Huairou Commission.

Li, Victor. 2000. "What's in a Name? Questions of Globalization." *Cultural Critique* 45:1–39.

Licona, Adela. 2005. "(B)orderlands' Rhetorics and Representations: The Transformative Potential of Feminist Third-Space Scholarship and Zines." *NWSA Journal* 17 (2): 104–29.

Liebowitz, Debra. J. 2002. "Gendering (Trans)National Advocacy." *International Feminist Journal of Politics* 4, no. 2 (August): 173–96.

Little, Peter D. 2001. "The Global Dimensions of Cross-Border Trade in the Somalia Borderlands." In *Globalization, Democracy and Development in Africa: Future Prospects,* edited by Abdel Gaffar M. Ahmed, 179–200. Addis Ababa: OSSREA.

Luckman, Susan. 1999. "(En)gendering the Digital Body: Feminism and the Internet." *Hecate* 25 (2): 36–48.

Macamo, Jose Luis. 1999. *Estimates of Unrecorded Cross-Border Trade between Mozambique and Her Neighbors.* Technical Paper No. 88, SD Publication Series, USAID, Washington DC.

Mahmood, Saba. 2005. *Politics of Piety: The Islamic Revival and the Feminist Subject.* Princeton, NJ: Princeton University Press.

Mamadouh, Virginie. 2004. "The North South Digital Divide in Transnational Grassroots Networks: Open Publishing and the Indymedia Network." Paper presented at the ICTs and Inequalities: The Digital Divides conference, Paris, November 18–19.

Marchand, Marianne H. 2003. "Challenging Globalisation: Feminism and Resistance." *Review of International Studies* 29 (3): 145–60.

Marchand, Marianne H., and Anne Sisson Runyan, eds. 2000. *Gender and Global Restructuring: Sightings, Sites and Resistances.* London: Routledge.

Marjit, S., and D. S. Maiti. 2005. *Globalization, Reform and the Informal Sector.* WIDER Research Paper No. 2005/12. UNU-WIDER. www.wider.unu.edu/publications/working-papers/research-papers/2005/en_GB/rp2005-12/, accessed April 6, 2006.

Martinez, Andrea, and Elizabeth Turcotte. 2003. "The Rise of Aboriginal Women's Global Connectivity," pp. 270–93 in Andrea Martinez and Meryn Stuart, eds. *Out of the Ivory Tower: Taking Feminist Research to the Community.* Toronto: Sumach Press.

McDonald, David, John Gay, Lovemore Zinyama, Robert Matter, and Fion de Vletter. 1998. *Challenging Xenophobia: Myths and Realities about Cross Border Migration in Southern Africa.* South African Migration Project Series Paper No. 7, at www.queensu.ca/samp/, accessed April 6, 2006.

McDonald, Kevin. 2006. *Global Movements: Action and Culture.* Malden, MA: Blackwell.

McLaughlin, L. 2004. "Feminism and the Political Economy of Transnational Public Space." *Sociological Review* 52 (1s): 156–75.

McMichael, Phillip. 2005. "Globalization and Development Studies." In *Critical Globalization Studies*, edited by Richard P. Appelbaum and William I. Robinson, 111–20. New York: Routledge.

Meadows, Michael, Susan Forde, and Kerry Foxwell. 2002. "Communicating Culture: Community Media in Australia." Paper presented at the Our Media, Not Theirs II conference, Barcelona, Spain.

Meikle, Graham. 2002. *Future Active: Media Activism and the Internet*. London: Routledge.

Mendoza, Breny. 2002. "Transnational Feminisms in Question." *Feminist Theory* 3 (3): 295–314.

Menon, Gayatri. 2001. *The Grassroots Women's International Academy at Expo 2000: Linking Living and Learning Communities from the Ground Up*. New York: Huairou Commission.

Minde, I. J., and T. O. Nakhumwa. 1998. *Unrecorded Cross-Border Trade between Malawi and Neighboring Countries*. Technical Paper No. 90, SD Publication Series, USAID, Washington DC.

Mittelman, James. 2005. "What is a Critical Globalization Studies." In *Critical Globalization Studies*, edited by Richard P. Appelbaum and William I. Robinson, 19–32. New York: Routledge.

Moghadam, Valentine. 2005. *Globalizing Women: Feminist Transnational Networks*. Baltimore, MD: The Johns Hopkins University Press.

———. 2003. "Is the Future of Revolution Feminist? Rewriting 'Gender and Revolutions' for a Globalizing World." In *The Future of Revolutions: Rethinking Radical Change in the Age of Globalization*, edited by John Foran, 159–68. London: Zed Books.

———. 2000. "Transnational Feminist Networks: Collective Action in an Era of Globalization." *International Sociology* 15 (1): 57–85.

Morris, Gayle, and John A. Dadson. 2000. "Ghana: Cross Border Trade Issues." Discussion Paper No. 22, African Economic Policy Papers, USAID, Washington DC.

Morris, Gayle, and Mahir Saul. 2005. "Women Cross-Border Traders in West Africa." In *Women in African Development: The Challenges of Globalization and Liberalization in the 21st Century*, edited by Sylvain Boko, Mina Baliamoune-Lutz, and Sitawa Kimuna, 53–82. Trenton, NJ: Africa World Press.

Mullings, Beverly. 2005. "Women Rule? Globalization and the Feminization of Managerial and Professional Workspaces in the Caribbean." *Gender, Place, and Culture* 12 (1): 1–27.

Murshid, K. A. S., and Tuot Sokphally. 2005. *The Cross Border Economies of Cambodia, Laos, Thailand and Vietnam*. Development Analysis Network. Phnom Penh, Cambodia.

Muzvidziwa, Victor. 2001 "Cross-Border Women Traders: Multiple Identities and Responses to New Challenges." *Journal of Contemporary African Studies* 19 (1): 67–80.

Namjoshi, Suniti. 1999. "A Meme of Great Power or What God Vishnu Has to Do with the Internet." In *Cyberfeminism: Connectivity, Critique and Creativity*, edited by Susan Hawthorne and Renate Klein, 372–80. North Melbourne, Australia: Spinifex Press.

Naples, Nancy A., and Manisha Desai. 2002. *Women's Activism and Globalization: Linking Local Struggles and Transnational Politics.* New York: Routledge.

Nash, June, and Maria P. Fernandez-Kelly, eds. 1983. *Women, Men and the International Division of Labor.* Albany, NY: SUNY Press.

Nederveen Pieterse, Jan. 2007. *Ethnicities and Global Multiculture: Pants for an Octopus.* Lanham, MD: Rowman & Littlefield.

———. 2006. "Emancipatory Cosmopolitanism: Towards an Agenda." Paper presented at the Cosmopolitanism: Exploring the Frontiers of Justice conference, The Hague, March 10.

———. 2004 *Globalization and Culture: Global Mélange.* Lanham, MD: Rowman & Littlefield.

Ong, Aihwa. 1999. *Flexible Citizenship: Cultural Logics of Transnationality.* Durham, NC: Duke University Press.

Ortellado, Pablo. 2002. "Combining Digital Technology and Traditional Media to Create Cooperative and Participatory Forms of Communication." Paper presented at the Our Media, Not Theirs II conference, Barcelona, Spain.

Osirim, Mary. 2003. "Carrying the Burden of Adjustment and Globalization: Women and Microenterprise Development in Urban Zimbabwe." *International Sociology* 18 (3): 535–58.

Pearson, Ruth. 2004. "The Social is Political." *International Feminist Journal of Politics* 6 (4): 603–22.

———. 2003. "Feminist Responses to Economic Globalization." In *Women Reinventing Globalization,* edited by Joanna Kerr and Caroline Sweetman, 25–34. Oxford: Oxfam.

Peberdy, Sally. 2002. "Hurdles to Trade? South Africa's Immigration Policy and Informal Sector Cross-Border Traders in the SADC." Paper presented at the SAMP/LHR/HSRC Workshop on Regional Integration, Poverty and South Africa's Proposed Migration Policy, Pretoria, April 23.

———. 2000. "Mobile Entrepreneurship: Informal Sector Cross-Border Trade and Street Trade in South Africa." *Development Southern Africa* 17 (2): 201–19.

Peberdy, Sally, and Jonathan Crush. 1998. *Trading Places: Cross Border Traders and the S. African Informal Sector.* South African Migration Policy Series, Paper No. 6, at www.queensu.ca/samp/, accessed April 6, 2006.

Peberdy, Sally, and Christian Rogerson. 2000. "Transnationalism and Non-South African Entrepreneurs in South Africa's Small, Medium, and Micro-Enterprise (SMME) Economy." *Canadian Journal of African Studies* 34 (1): 20–40.

Peters, Fabienne. 2003. "Gender and the Foundations of Social Choice: The Role of Situated Agency." *Feminist Economic* 9 (3): 13–32.

Piper, Nicola, and Anders Uhlin, eds. 2004. *Transnational Activism in Asia: Problems of Power and Democracy.* London: Routledge.

Plant, Sadie. 1997. *Zeros + Ones: Digital Women + the New Technoculture.* New York: Doubleday.

Platon Sara, and Mark Deluze. 2003. "IndyMedia Journalism: A Radical Way of Making, Selecting, and Sharing News?" *Journalism* 4 (3): 336–55.

Plunkett, Daniel J., and J. Dirck Stryker. 2002. *Regional Interventions to Improve Cross-Border Trade and Food Security in West Africa.* USAID AFR/SD Agricultural Policy Development Program, USAID, Washington DC.

Poster, Winifred, and Zakia Salime. 2002. "The Limits of Microcredit: Transnational Feminism and USAID Activities in the United States and Morocco." In *Women's Activism and Globalization: Linking Local Struggles and Transnational Politics,* edited by Nancy A. Naples and Manisha Desai, 189–219. New York: Routledge.

Pourtier, Roland. 2003. *Central Africa and the Cross-Border Regions: Reconstruction and Integration Prospects.* Initiative for Central Africa, USAID, Washington DC.

Primo, Natasha. 2003. *Gender Issues in the Information Society.* Paris: UNESCO.

Proenza, Francisco J., Roberto Bastidas-Buch, and Guillermo Montero. 2001. *Telecenters for Socio-Economic and Rural Development in Latin America and the Caribbean.* Washington, DC: FAO-ITU-IADB.

Prugl, Elisabeth. 1999. *The Global Construction of Gender: Home-Based Work in the Political Economy of the 20th Century.* New York: Columbia University Press.

Pyle, Jean. 2006. "Globalization, Transnational Migration, and Gendered Care Work: An Introduction." *Globalizations* 3 (3): 286–96.

Qvortrup, Lars. 1989. "The Nordic Telecottages." *Telecommunications Policy*, March: 59–68.

Rai, Shirin. 2004. "Gendering Global Governance." *International Feminist Journal of Politics* 6 (4): 579–601.

Rees, T. 2005. "Reflections on the Uneven Development of Gender Mainstreaming." *International Feminist Journal of Politics* 7 (4): 555–74.

Ricciutelli, Luciana, Angela Rose Miles, and Margaret McFadden. 2004. *Feminist Politics, Activism and Vision: Local and Global Challenges.* London: Palgrave Macmillan.

Ritzer, George. 2004. *The Globalization of Nothing.* Thousand Oaks, CA: Sage.

———. 1993. *The McDonaldization of Society.* Thousand Oaks, CA: Pine Forge Press.

Robertson, Roland. 1992. *Globalization: Social Theory and Global Culture.* London: Sage. .

Robins, Melinda. 2002. "Are African Women Online Just ICT Consumers?" *Gazette,* Vol. 64, No. 3, 235–249.

Robinson, William I. 2005, "What Is a Critical Globalization Studies? Intellectual Labor and Global Society." In *Critical Globalization Studies,* edited by Richard P. Appelbaum and William I. Robinson, 11–18. New York: Routledge.

Rodriguez, Clemencia. 2001. *Fissures in the Mediascape: An International Study of Citizens' Media.* Creskill, NJ: Hampton Press.

Russell, Nathan. 2004. "Is There an 'E' in 'Scaling Up'? Lessons from a Community Telecenter in Southwestern Colombia." In *Scaling Up and Out: Achieving Widespread Impact through Agricultural Research,* edited by Douglas Pachico and Sam Fujisaka, 211–20. CIAT. Cali, Colombia.

Salzinger, Leslie. 2004. "From Gender as Object to Gender as Verb: Rethinking How Global Restructuring Happens." *Critical Sociology* 30 (1): 43–62.

Sarvasy, Wendy, and Patrizia Longo. 2004. "Kant's World Citizenship and Filipina Migrant Domestics." *International Feminist Journal of Politics* 6 (3): 392–415.

Sassen, Saskia. 2006. *Sociology of Globalization.* New York: Norton.

———. 2004. "Local Actors in Global Politics." *Current Sociology* 52 (4): 649–70.

———. 2000. "Women's Burden: Counter-Geographies of Globalization and the Feminization of Survival." *Journal of International Affairs* 53 (2): 504–24.

Scholte, Jan Aart. 2002. "Civil Society and Democracy in Global Governance." *Global Governance* 8(3): 281–304.

———. 2000. *Globalization: A Critical Introduction*. London: Macmillan.

Seidman, Gay W. 2000. "Adjusting the Lens: What do Globalizations, Transnationalism, and the Anti-apartheid Movement Mean for Social Movement Theory?" In *Globalizations and Social Movements: Culture, Power and the Transnational Public Sphere*, edited by John A. Guidry, Michael D. Kennedy, and Mayer N. Zald, 339–57. Ann Arbor: University of Michigan Press.

Sen, Gita. 2005. *Neolibs, Neocons and Gender Justice: Lessons from Global Negotiations*. Geneva: UNRISD.

Simon-Kumar, Rachel. 2004. "Negotiating Emancipation: Public Sphere, Gender, and Critiques of Neo-liberalism." *International Feminist Journal of Politics* 6 (3): 485–506.

Simpson, L., L. Daws, and B. Pini. 2004. "Public Internet Access Revisited." *Telecommunications Policy* 28 (3–4): 323–37.

Sinha, Mrinalini, Donna Guy, and Angela Woollacott, eds., 1999. *Feminisms and Internationalism*. Oxford: Blackwell.

Sklair, Leslie. 2005. "Generic Globalization, Capitalist Globalization and Beyond: A Framework for Critical Globalization Studies." In *Critical Globalization Studies*, edited by Richard P. Appelbaum and William I. Robinson, 55–64. New York: Routledge.

———. 2002. *Globalization: Capitalism and Its Alternatives*. Oxford: Oxford University Press.

Society for International Development. 2003. *Politics, Culture, and Justice: Women and the Politics of Place*. Rome.

Soros, George. 2002. *George Soros on Globalization*. New York: Public Affairs.

Spender, Dale. 1995. *Nattering on the Net*. Melbourne: Spinifex Press.

Stack, Carol. 1997. *All Our Kin*. New York: Basic Books.

Steger, Manfred B. 2003. *Globalization: A Very Short Introduction*. Oxford: Oxford University Press.

Stevenson, Nick. 2003. *Cultural Citizenship: Cosmopolitan Questions*. Maidenhead, Berkshire: Open University Press.

Stiglitz, Joseph. 2002. *Globalization and Its Discontents*. New York: Norton.

Surman, Mark. 2004. *Commonspace: Beyond Virtual Community*. Commons Group, at commons.ca/articles/fulltext.shtml?x=347.

Tarrow, Sidney. 2005. *The New Transnational Activism*. Cambridge, UK: Cambridge University Press.

Tiberghien, Chan. 2004. "Gender-Skepticism or Gender Boom? Poststructural Feminisms and the World Conference Against Racism." *International Feminist Journal of Politics* 6 (3): 454–84.

Turkle, Sherry. 1995. *Life on the Screen: Identity in the Age of the Internet*. New York: Simon & Schuster.

Uganda Bureau of Statistics. 2004. *The Informal Cross Border Trade Survey Report*. Entebbe.

United Nations. www.un.org.

United Nations Development Fund for Women. www.unifem.org/.

Urry, John. 2003. *Global Complexity*, London: Polity.

Vargas, Virginia. 2003. "Feminism, Globalization, and the Global Justice and Solidarity Movement." *Cultural Studies* 17 (6): 905–20.

Vatikiotis, Pantelis. 2004. "Communication Theory and Alternative Media." *Westminster Papers in Communication and Culture* 1 (2): 4–29.

Voicu, Ioan. 2004. "From Digital Divide to Global Digital Solidarity" *ABAC Journal* 24 (1): 1–46.

Walby, Sylvia. 2005. "Gender Mainstreaming: Productive Tension in Theory and Practice." *Social Politics* 12 (3): 321–43.

——. 2001. "From Community to Coalition: The Politics of Recognition as the Handmaiden to the Politics of Equality in an Era of Globalization." *Theory, Culture, and Society* 18 (2–3): 113–35.

Wallerstein, Immanuel. 2004. *World System Analysis: An Introduction*. Durham, NC: Duke University Press.

Walzer, Michael, ed. 1997. *Toward a Global Civil Society*. Oxford: Berghahn Books.

Ward, Kathryn. 1990. *Women Workers and Global Restructuring*. Ithaca, NY: Cornell University Press.

Waring, Marilyn. 2003. "Counting for Something: Recognizing Women's Contributions to the Global Economy through Alternative Accounting Systems." In *Women Reinventing Globalization*, edited by Joanna Kerr and Caroline Sweetman, 35–43. Oxford: Oxfam.

Waterman, Peter. 2002. *Globalization, Social Movements and the New Internationalisms*. 2nd ed. London: Continuum.

Whiteside, Martin. 1998. *When the Whole Is More Than the Sum of the Parts: The Effect of Cross-Border Interactions on Livelihood Security in Southern Malawi and Northern Mozambique*. Report for Oxfam GB, Oxford.

Williams, Raymond. 1963. *Culture and Society*. New York: Columbia University Press.

Wolf, Martin. 2004. *Why Globalization Works*. New Haven, CT: Yale University Press.

Women in Informal Employment: Globalizing and Organizing. 2001. *Annual Report*. www.wiego.org, accessed April 6, 2006.

Wright, Eric O. 2006. "Real Utopias." Paper presented at the Transnational Seminar Series, University of Illinois, Urbana-Champaign, September.

www.un.org/womenwatch/daw/csw/index.html. Report of the 49th Session. Accessed April 2006.

Youngs, Gillian. 2006. "Gender and Technology: The Internet in Context." In *The Ideology of the Internet: Concepts, Policies, Uses*, edited by K. Sarikakis and D. K. Thussu, 47–61. New York: Hampton Press.

——. 2005. "Ethics of Access: Globalization, Feminism and Information Society." *Journal of Global Ethics* 1 (1): 69–84.

——. 2004. "Cyberspace: The New Feminist Frontier?" In *Women and Media: International Perspectives*, edited by Karen Ross and Carolyn Byerly, 185–208. Malden, MA: Blackwell.

——. 2002. "Feminizing Cyberspace: Rethinking Technoagency." In *Rethinking Empowerment: Gender and Development in a Global/Local World*, edited by Jane L. Parpart, Shirin M. Rai, and Kathleen Staudt, 79–94. London: Routledge.

——. 1998. "Virtual Voices: Real Lives." In *Women@Internet: Creating New Cultures in Cyberspace*, edited by Wendy Harcourt, 55–68. London: Zed Books.

YUVA. www.yuvaindia.org/.

Yuval-Davis, Nira. 2006. "Intersectionality and Feminist Politics." *European Journal of Women's Studies* 13 (3): 193–209.

Zimmerman, Mary K., Jacquelyn S. Litt, and Christina E. Bose. 2006. *Global Dimensions of Gender and Carework*. Palo Alto, CA: Stanford University Press.

Index

Acker, Joan, 4
Afghanistan, 74
Africa, 4, 7, 17, 32, 34, 50, 55n3, 65, 73, 92; client networks in, 24; cross-border trade in, 15, 19, 20, 21; and globalization, 14; HIV/AIDS in, 26, 42; households in, and women, 15; informal work in, 16
African Women's Development and Communication Network (FEMNET), 56n16
Agencia Latinoamericana de Informacion (Latin American Information Agency; ALAI): advocacy, promoting of, 81; collective spaces, providing for, 84; and Internet, 80
agency, 30n4
alternative media, 72
Americanization, 60
Angola, 1
antiglobalization, 49
Anzaldua, Gloria, 60
Area Mujeres (Women's Programme), 80, 84; and Internet access, 81
Argentina, 80; Independent Media Centers (IMCs) in, 75, 76; Internet in, 76

Arinson, Mathew, 68
Articulacion Feminista Marcosur (AFM), 56n16
Asia, 4, 11n3, 23, 32, 34, 43, 44, 46, 50, 55n3, 78; elite women traders in, 20; informal work in, 16
Asia West Pacific Network for Urban Conservation (AWPNUC), 45
Asian Women and Shelter Network, 41
assimilationist hybridity, 60
Association for Progressive Communications (APC), 37, 80, 84; and gender inequality, 77
Australia, 70, 77; IMCs in, 73

Bangladesh, 30n3
Beijing (China), 35
Beijing Conference, 8, 36, 38
Beijing Platform for Action, 37; gender equality, and men, role of in, 38
Benin, 20, 28
blogs, 91
Bolivia, 75, 85
Bombay (India), 44, 50; youth movement in, 48. *See also* Mumbai (India)
border residents: border identity, as place-based, 28

113

About the Author

Manisha Desai is the director of women's studies and associate professor of sociology at the University of Connecticut. From 2002 to 2007, she was with the Women and Gender in Global Perspectives Program and the Department of Sociology at the University of Illinois, Urbana-Champaign, and from 1990 to 2002 she was with Hobart and William Smith Colleges in Geneva, New York. In addition to her academic positions, she has served as the senior program specialist at the Gender, Equity, and Development section at UNESCO in Paris.

Her areas of research and teaching include transnational feminisms, gender and globalization, gender and development, women's human rights, and contemporary Indian society. Her research has led to the publication of numerous articles, book chapters, and the following books: *Gender, Family, and Law in a Globalizing Middle East and South Asia*, coedited with Ken Cuno (2009); *Women's Issues in Asia and Oceania* (2003); *Women's Activism and Globalization: Linking Local Struggles to Transnational Politics*, coedited with Nancy Naples (2002).

She is the past president of Sociologists for Women in Society (SWS) having served as its president in 2007. She has represented SWS at the UN's Economic and Social Council and serves on the International Council of Sociologists Without Borders and on the board of the *International Feminist Journal of Politics*.